The Book of

POSTCARD COLLECTING

N. Y. 11 Future New York
"The city of skyscrapers"

© MOSES KING

The Book of
POSTCARD
COLLECTING

Thomas E. Range

E. P. Dutton ‖ New York

For information contact: E. P. Dutton, 2 Park Avenue, New York, N.Y. 10016

Library of Congress Catalog Card Number: 78-75289

ISBN: 0-525-93157-0

Published simultaneously in Canada by Clarke, Irwin & Company Limited, Toronto and Vancouver

10 9 8 7 6 5 4 3 2 1

First Edition

Book design by George H. Buehler/Blair McFadden

To Elizabeth Ann Seton, for her help

Contents

Color insert follows page 96

Acknowledgments

The author wishes to express his appreciation to his friends and fellow collectors, whose assistance and encouragement have added to the enjoyment of producing this guide to collecting picture postcards.

First and foremost, I thank Rita G. Schaf, whose typing skills, enthusiasm, and ideas have contributed immeasurably to the production of this book. Others to whom special thanks are extended include George Guzzio and Louis Blumengarten for their kind permission to use cards from their collections as illustrations, as credited below; Paul Allersmeyer for his enthusiasm and support; Betty Davis for access to her extensive private library of deltiological publications; John McClintock for his thoughts on postcard exhibiting; Barker Gummer, the patient librarian of the Washington's Crossing Card Collectors Club; and Allen Wright, the friend and dealer who introduced me to postcard collecting long before I realized how much fun it would be.

Picture Credits

The author gratefully acknowledges the assistance of his friends in their permission to reproduce cards from their collections, as follows:

Courtesy Louis Blumengarten: Figures 25, 92, 146, 167, 173, 174, 187, 188, 197, 198, 201, 202, 203.

Courtesy George Guzzio: Figures 8, 93, 107, 121, 123, 124, 176, 208, 218; plates 4, 6, 17, 18, 29.

The Book of

POSTCARD COLLECTING

Introduction

A few years ago, I received a phone call from a good friend and fellow stamp collector. He had acquired a quantity of old picture postcards from a local antiques dealer and wondered if we could inspect the cards together, looking for interesting postage stamps and unusual cancellations. As both of us were lifelong stamp collectors, we were seldom interested in the picture appearing on the front of the card. Our review of the cards for philatelic appeal was disappointing—nothing much in the way of stamps or cancellations of interest to philatelists. Then we turned the cards over.

Each card depicted a scene of our hometown: photographs taken around the turn of the century by major photographic studios, produced by the card publishers for sale to the tourist or traveler so that he could convey his message of joy or loneliness to his family and friends. The cards showed buildings long since destroyed under the wrecker's ball, trolleys that I vaguely remembered riding as a boy, stores and homes long since sacrificed to street widening and the parking needs of the modern motorist, a church that was old at the time the card was published and somehow survived futile attempts at "modernization," and automobiles long since relegated to museums, filled with happy families on a day's outing. And the people—shoppers strolling along a busy thoroughfare; policemen in their Keystone Kops conical helmets; firemen tending their horse-drawn, steam-driven pumpers; farmers, tradesmen, street vendors, families taking their ease in parks and at recreation piers, shop girls, stevedores, stockbrokers—all of them were portrayed on these cardboard mirrors of our past.

Another stamp-collecting friend introduced me to a club of postcard collectors, dozens of people who shared my enthusiasm for what was to me a new field of collecting. Through these friends and the club's publications, I learned the history of postcards: their origins in Europe and the spread of postcard production to America at the turn of the century; the techniques and science of collecting, or what to buy and where to buy it; the fascinating study of the backs of the postcards; and the sources of reference works to find out the history of the subject shown on a card. My collecting friends pointed out the different disciplines of collecting: acquiring cards of a particular publisher; cards illustrated by drawings of particular artists who signed their postcard illustrations much as a painter does his canvas; cards commemorating expositions and world's fairs; series of cards featuring the days of the week, the four seasons, the months of the year; cards illustrating Indians, blacks, Orientals; cards mailed to wish people Merry Christmas, Happy New Year, Happy Thanksgiving; cards showing farms and cities, mansions and ghettos, the rich, the poor, the native, the immigrant; cards depicting drawings from history, Lincoln's birthplace, the site of Washington's inauguration, Colonial settlements; cards showing the construction of skyscrapers and bridges and the destruction of cities from earthquakes, flood, and conflagration.

I was shown entire collections of cards showing different views of the same subject, like the Statue of Liberty and New York's Flat Iron Building; collections of pictures of horse-drawn vehicles, covered bridges, lighthouses, factories, railroads, sailing ships, steamships, airships; cards featuring presidents, governors, royalty, military figures; geographical collections devoted to cities such as Philadelphia, Washington, Chicago, San Francisco, ever changing over the decades; and cards showing the small towns of the country whose residents take rightful pride in the little-changing quaintness and hospitality of their communities. It seemed that each member collected what he wanted without a slavish reliance on a catalogue or album page.

Faced with the myriad choices of material available, I decided in short order what my specialty would be: my hometown, New York City. In 1900, Manhattan was a ferryboat ride from the farms of New Jersey; it has its history as the first capital of the United States; it served as the home office of many of the giant industrial and commercial companies. Its architectural wonders are world-renowned. It was and is a tourist attraction for world travelers and was the port of entry for millions of immigrants, who sent picture postcards to their friends in the old country. This book, as a consequence, has a liberal sprinkling of illustrative cards from my collection picturing New York subjects. But other sections of the country, featuring points of interest peculiar to these parts, will also be represented: the ice-clad Niagara Falls, rural railroad stations, the dreamy inactivity of a small town Main Street, the lakeshore estates of the rich, the tragedy of the San Francisco earthquake and fire.

Through the club and its members, it was relatively easy to obtain the postcards I was interested in. The next step in this most enjoyable hobby was to find out as much as possible about the card's subject. In many cases, enough information appeared on the card to give a clue as to the subject or the location of the view. Fellow members were helpful in identification. But for the most part, it took hours of digging into seventy-year-old reference works, portfolios of old photographs, newspaper articles, biographies, and historical works. The results were most rewarding. Not only did I learn about my chosen topic of interest—the postcards of New York—but about the 300-year history of the city itself. What a boon such research would have been twenty-five years ago as I struggled through history exams in high school!

I learned that the old church that survived in the busiest commercial district is St. Paul's Chapel, built in 1766, at which George Washington worshiped on the day of his inauguration as the first president and during his term while New York City was the nation's capital. My research delved into the history of automobiles, electricity, subway and elevated systems, architecture and architects, and the development of the skyscraper. It has touched upon the engineering achievements represented by the construction of bridges and tunnels, the transformation of the shipping industry from sail to steam, the evolution of the aircraft industry. And as in most research, the answer to one question has raised half a dozen more. Why was a particular building erected on a particular site? Who designed it? When was it constructed? What caused its destruction? What preceded the building at this location? What succeeded it? Such questions arise no matter what subject is being researched.

The cards used to illustrate this book represent a good cross section of the multiplicity of collecting interests available to a postcard collector. In these pages will be found examples of different postcard "backs" through which the development of postal regulations can be traced. Cards bearing interesting messages are included, even though they might obscure portions of the cards' designs. Cards that were employed for curious usages—such as notifications of club meetings and a boycott of publications—are included. Cards printed in foreign countries for a foreign market but picturing American scenes can be found here. And an amazing item: a card showing a view of New York's Herald Square that was mailed to Illinois from a city in Tibet!

All these illustrations and the narrative will, I hope, convince the reader of the joys of collecting picture postcards.

1

Obtaining the Material

The Philatelic Connection

The formal and systematized collecting of picture postcards should not be an alien concept to anyone familiar with the elements of stamp collecting. A common ground between the two disciplines is the maximum card, a picture postcard to which a stamp of the same design is affixed and to which a first day or fancy cancellation has been applied to "tie" the stamp to the card. See Figure 1. Maximum cards have been prepared for use on first days of issue of similarly designed stamps for decades.

Figure 1. postmarked 1970.

In most cases, the philatelist places emphasis on the stamp and the cancellation; the card is of itself relatively unimportant. To a card collector, the card is paramount; in fact, he might deplore the card's being "ruined" by the stamp and cancellation appearing on the pretty picture.

As there is this common ground between the two hobbies, a postcard collector should start his quest for material at stamp dealers, especially those who handle or specialize in covers (that is, envelopes to which stamps are affixed and canceled) or postal stationery (the postal cards and stamped envelopes issued by the post office). Announce to him that you collect picture postcards and that you'd like to see a selection. After a quizzical stare, as he wonders why anyone wastes his time collecting postcards, he might rummage through some old shoe boxes and come up with a supply. Most stamp dealers know very little of the value of cards; in his dusty shoe box might be some better cards at a reasonable price. Conversely there might be some mediocre cards priced high, reflecting the value of the stamps or a cancellation appearing thereon. Too often, a card collector has to pay through the nose for a card merely because a good U.S. commemorative or an important cancellation appears on the address side.

Beware the unpriced card! Reputable dealers price each item they are selling or label a box "all 25¢." An unsuspecting collector can be taken advantage of when, after he has made his selection, the dealer sets a high price, knowing the collector's interest. Talk price before going through a box, and if the dealer is not willing to set ground rules, walk away. The Yellow Pages under "Stamps for Collectors" list stamp dealers in your area.

Antiques Mean Old Postcards Too

An antiques dealer is as apt to acquire a stock of postcards as a stamp dealer, perhaps even more so as there are relatively few stamp dealers interested in relegating selling space to what is to them low markup material. The most collectible of postcards are from the 1900s and probably have been hidden away all these years in the drawer of the antique desk that the dealer is trying to sell. If he handles enough desks, he can accumulate quite a few cards. This should be ripe pickings for the card collector—material considered superfluous by the dealer and stored in a junk box priced to move. Since the cards came with the desk, what they bring in resale is found money.

For some reason, postcards in a beat-up old album are always assumed to have more value. It probably means that a youngster was given an album for Christmas seventy years ago and spent a week trying to maneuver his cards into those little die-cut slots without bending the corners. (The relative merits of the use of albums are discussed in chapter 9.) So don't place any particular importance on a card just because of its appearance in an album; the dealer could have been stocking the album the night before with items from his junk box. And you're buying the whole card, not just the front or picture side. Always take a look at the back of the card. The Yellow Pages give a listing of antiques dealers, of course.

Flea Markets Do Not Sell Fleas

There are few areas in the country that do not feature a flea market at some time during the year. A flea market is a combination of a church bazaar, a garage sale, a county fair, and a rummage sale that attracts dealers of practically every sort of merchandise. It is generally held in a farmer's field or a parking lot. The card in figure 2 publicizes the Lambertville, New Jersey, Antique Flea Market, typical of the thousands of markets dotting America's countryside, at which postcards are generally available.

Pickup trucks filled with merchandise start arriving at the more popular markets in early morning darkness, the dealers groping around with flashlights looking for the piece of ground they have rented for the day or the weekend.

Figure 2. c. 1970.

There is bound to be at least one dealer with a supply of postcards, usually priced low for quick turnover. Dealers have to be able to sell out at these markets, using the proceeds to obtain new material for the next weekend's market, perhaps being held 200 or 300 miles away. As flea market dealers are generalists, handling any kind of material from which they feel a dollar can be made, they are less apt to realize the true value of whatever cards pass through their hands. So good buys can be found and the dealers are more inclined to bargain. Don't ever be embarrassed to engage in the timeless tactic of offering much less than the asking price for items you want. Flea market dealers expect this and probably welcome the give-and-take session. Of course, the professional postcard dealers and more advanced collectors are aware of the bargain cards available at flea markets, and they will be out there in the fields with their flashlights looking through the merchandise as the parked pickup trucks are being unloaded.

The flea market is probably the only source of postcards for the rural or suburban collector who is not inclined to travel to established dealers and antique shops. A glance at your local newspaper will uncover ads for the markets. Go to as many as you can; they represent a day's enjoyment even if you never find a postcard.

The Corner Drugstore

There is no rule that a postcard collection has to contain old cards. Certainly this book does not contain that statement. A collection should reflect the interest of the collector and should be started with a view to pure enjoyment, relaxation, and personal satisfaction. What better and more convenient source of cards could there be than the rack at the local drugstore, card shop, or variety store. Figure 3, produced as an advertisement by Wyco Products, displays the publisher's products on the familiar wall and rotary racks appearing in many local shops.

Figure 3. c. 1970.

There are few locations in the country that have been overlooked by the peripatetic eye of the commercial photographer's camera. The local church, the main street, the restaurants, motels, and hotels in your neighborhood are bound to appear on cards commercially available. Pick the racks clean of one of each view, pay the man the dollar or two it costs, and go home in the realization that you have just started your postcard collection. Or better yet, don't go home but seek out the building or view depicted on the card to see if it is still there. In this fast-changing age, the peaceful farm scene on a postcard a few years old may have been transformed into the latest shopping center. What is even more fun is to find the shopping center on a card, thereby having a nice "before-and-after" duo. Make note of the postcard publisher's name, which usually appears on the back of the card. Probably he is a local photographer; look him up in the phone book and ask him what other cards he has produced and whether they are available. Get his price list and fill in the cards you may be missing. If the publisher has been in business for a while, he may have earlier views of the subjects appearing on his current cards. That peaceful farm scene may show up without that post–World War II silo and barn, and if you are lucky, some farm machinery and an old auto or two may appear on the older view. The inclusion of people, vehicles, and activity in a scene makes for a more interesting card, not only to you but to other collectors whose interests are specialized in these topics.

Grandma's Attic, Friends, Neighbors, and Other Sources

A popular gift for a youngster during the postcard craze of seventy years ago was a batch of cards—possibly complete sets of various subjects—and an album to put them in. Postcards were as popular for gift giving as, say, phonograph records and tapes are today, and they served the same purpose: to keep the little dears out of the adult's hair. The prudent child of the 1900s saved the cards given him, traded unwanted cards with friends, and mailed them to other collectors with similar interests, and as time passed, they were put away with other childhood possessions. More likely, the child's mother lovingly tucked away in a trunk the postcard album with the teddy bears, dolls, toy soldiers, and other artifacts of youth. Three generations later, after world wars, depressions, recessions, and relative good times, someone in the family remembers Grandma's attic and the postcard album. With a little luck, it will be your Grandma's postcards.

Do not hesitate to mention your collecting interests to your friends and neighbors. After the same type of quizzical stare the stamp dealer gave you, they might remember the batch of cards they brought back with them from the world's fair or Disneyland. They might be happy to pass them along to you. Never refuse any card offered to you; not only might it hurt the feelings of the donor, but it will probably spoil the chances of your ever being offered cards again.

Always take advantage of your business or vacation trips, picking up whatever cards are available en route. If driving, get off the main highways occasionally and drive through some of the small towns to see what their stores have to offer. A half-hour layover in the train station or airport terminal will give you the opportunity of grabbing up one of each card displayed on the racks. There is no shortage of cards or sources of them. Gathering up cards depends only on your ingenuity in seeking them out.

A Postcard Collectors' Club

In your discussions with dealers and with other collectors you come in contact with, you might hear of a local card collectors' club. For the serious collector, membership in a club is a must. Nowhere else will you get the exposure to expert advice and quality material that you will get from the members and dealers who attend the periodic meetings. While the importance of postcard collectors' clubs is more fully covered in chapters 5 and 10, the value of such clubs to both novices and advanced collectors cannot be overemphasized.

Publicity cards, issued by two of the larger active postcard clubs, appear as figures 4 and 5. In figure 4, this club meets monthly in New York City and issues a bulletin to its members. The club in figure 5 holds monthly meetings in Elkhart,

Indiana, and publishes a club bulletin. Both of these postcards use in their designs reproductions of commercial cards that their club members would be interested in collecting.

Figure 4. 1971.

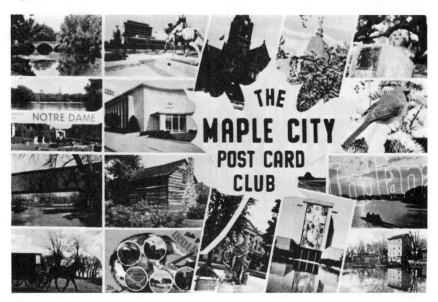

Figure 5. c. 1970.

Most clubs distribute to their members bulletins that might contain not only articles of general collecting interest but checklists of known cards in a series, book reviews of reference works, dealer advertisements, and tips on how to care for your cards. The meetings feature guest speakers and club-sponsored auctions in which members enter their excess material for bidding. You may discover that your farm scene appears on a card produced prior to May 19, 1898, when picture postcards were not specifically authorized by the U.S. Congress and had to pass through the mails at the two-cent price of a letter rather than the one-cent rate authorized after that date. You may find that the farm scene was used as a subject for a painting by one of the many artists who did contract work for the postcard publishers and whose name appears on his tiny illustration. The farm scene may also appear on a card produced just prior to March 1, 1907, when the sender was first allowed to write a message on the back of a card. In going through a dealer's box you may find the scene appearing in a black-and-white view, or in full color, or hand-tinted. It can be printed on a rough-textured paper or on glossy stock, depending on the time frame in which the card was produced.

Fellow collectors will apprise you of newspapers and magazines devoted to card collecting, copies of which can be borrowed from club members or from the club library. Note the dealers' ads in these publications; they will contain line after line of descriptions of cards offered for sale. Though many descriptions will be undecipherable at first, members will be happy to help in the translation. You may spot an ad for a selection of amusement parks, a popular topic, which you might consider purchasing to complement the Disneyland cards your neighbor gave you. Your farm scene might be included in a geographic grouping of the county in which it is located. Your card from the layover at the airport would go nicely with a selection of aircraft cards showing different types of planes spanning the years from the Wright brothers to the Concorde.

The Collector and the Dealer Should Be Friends

Be frank with the card dealers you will meet. They attend the meetings to serve the members in their collecting interests. Ask their help in selecting material and organizing a collection. A dealer wants you to buy, as much as you want to acquire material that strikes your fancy. He is constantly buying material from collectors and other dealers and will keep your interests in mind as cards pass through his hands. You will find that his stock is arranged in an order that will facilitate browsing. Airplane cards will be grouped in one spot; view cards will be sorted into states and perhaps counties, cities, and towns. Cards showing automobiles, ships, horse-drawn vehicles, patriotic subjects will all have their sections in the dealer's boxes. Generally, a dealer's memory of his material is phenomenal. Mention a particular subject and give him a few minutes and he will come up with a selection hidden away somewhere for which he has not had a request for months.

A dealer-member of a postcard collectors' club has his reputation to maintain. As he attends the club meetings month after month, his prices and the quality of his material have to remain fair and competitive with those of other dealers at the meeting. Word soon gets around about a dealer who is unethical in his transactions with customers, and when that happens, he will soon see only empty chairs at his table.

The Exhibitions

You will note either from announcements at the club or from your hobby reading material a number of postcard exhibitions held throughout the country during the year. These exhibitions, or shows, serve as a gathering place for thousands of collectors and dozens, if not scores, of dealers. Bring your checkbook, for the material you will be offered will be irresistible. Realize that these dealers have been accumulating stock specifically for sale at these shows and have incurred considerable traveling and lodging expenses. They will be loaded with cards that you have been looking for and were unable to find at the local dealers. Depending upon where you live, attendance at these shows could entail some traveling on your part—perhaps an overnight stay at the nearest motel. Many avid collectors make their vacation plans around shows presented in various parts of the country. The promoters of the shows realize this and schedule their shows in sequence so that a family living in, say, New Jersey can travel west to Ohio over a three-week period and "hit" three or four shows along the route. It makes for a fascinating vacation for a collector, provided he has an understanding spouse and family.

2

Evaluating the Material

Old Is Good

Using the various sources to obtain a quantity of cards, the obvious question is, Is this stuff any good? As a general rule, applicable to any type of collectibles, old is good. The easiest way to determine the age of a postcard is to turn it over to see if it was used, as evidenced by a postmark. Although a postmark determines that the card existed on the day it was mailed, the card naturally could have been used to send a message any time from the day it was printed up to yesterday. A 1948 postmark does not indicate that the card was produced in that year but rather that it existed in that year. The card could have been decades old before its use. Drawing upon a stamp collector's familiarity with stamps, the age of a card with an indistinct postmark (cancellation) can be determined by what stamp was used to mail it. There is, however, the same pitfall—an old stamp may have been used to mail an old card years after both were produced.

The best way to determine the age of a card is to become familiar with the styles of cards produced over the years and the all-important *backs*, that is, the address sides of the cards. The evolution of the backs of the cards is outlined and illustrated in chapter 3, "The Flip Side." The picture side of the card will be explored here. The early cards—by this is meant those produced from 1893 to 1907—had a space on the face for a brief message. This blank space could take from about a half or a third of a card to a half-inch strip useful for little more than the sender's name.

Figure 6, mailed in 1902, illustrates virtually the whole of the blank message space being utilized by the sender because in this period no message was al-

Figure 6. postmarked 1902.

lowed on the back. The card was produced by Arthur Strauss (No. 227) and shows New York's Williamsburg Bridge under construction. The bridge itself was completed in 1903.

Figure 7 is a view of the same bridge (although stylized—those little peaked tops on the towers were never built) issued by Koehler (No. 122), with a message squeezed into the stingy space permitted at that time by the postal authorities.

Figure 7. postmarked 1906.

Cards produced by Strauss and Koehler are sought after by many collectors, irrespective of the subjects appearing on the cards.

The space for a message on the front of the card—however small—usually indicates that a card was produced prior to March 1, 1907, the date when senders were allowed to write a message on the back.

The style of the card can be used to determine its age. Figure 8 is representative of the white bordered era stretching roughly from 1915 to 1930, during which millions of cards were mass-produced "on the cheap." Although this period is looked upon with distain by self-styled advanced collectors and dealers, it cannot be overlooked by anyone with an interest in the development of postcards.

This card is a rather commonplace view transformed into an interesting card by the inclusion of the Coca-Cola sign (on the roof of the building to the left) and those nice 1920s automobiles parked in front of the central building.

The products of the linen era are probably the most vilified of cards and in many cases justifiably so. This period represents the nadir in postcard production, with virtually no regard exercised on the part of the card companies for the aesthetic appeal of a card to a collector. The term *linen* is derived from the texture of the cardboard stock upon which the picture is produced. It is a rough cross-hatching not unlike linen cloth. The cheapest of inks can be applied to this type of stock—and they were! The 1930–1940 period, however, cannot be ignored and

CHIMNEY CORNER JUNCTION OF MIDLAND TRAIL (ROUTE 60) 19 AND 21, NEAR GAULEY BRIDGE, W. VA.   3A466

Figure 8. postmarked 1934.

written off. Consider the events that occurred in this period: the dawn of commercial aviation, the Great Depression, the decline in the use of the trolley and the corresponding increase in buses and automobiles, the 1939 World's Fair in New York City, and the girding for the trials of World War II.

America's cautious optimism is illustrated by figure 9, copyrighted in 1941, produced by Curt Teich (No. 3B-H703). This quasi-political–cum-patriotic theme symbolizes the country's emergence from the Depression and its assumption of the role as the guardian of democracy. This card, together with its companion piece figure 10, No. 3B-H704, copyrighted a year later, contains many subjects of interest to collectors. The presidential picture, the large letters, the flag, and the

Figure 9. 1941.

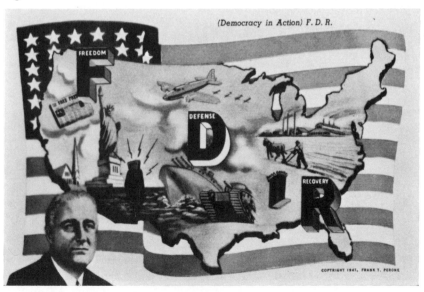

(Democracy in Action) F. D. R.

COPYRIGHT 1941, FRANK T. PERONE

(Arsenal of Democracy) U. S. A.

COPYRIGHT, 1942, FRANK T. PERONE

Figure 10. 1942.

symbolic objects within the outline of the country make these cards among the most interesting of the products of the linen era.

The beginning of the chrome era has been fixed by expert card historians in 1939 upon the issuance of a set of eighty-five cards in a promotional program by the Union Oil Company. Card Number 1, a scene of the Red Rock Country in Arizona, is shown in figure 11. It is postmarked Cottonwood, Ariz. June 21, 1939. The chrome era is so called because of the use of color photographic film for the direct reproduction of views onto postcard stock—the term being derived from the trade name *Kodachrome*. Union Oil used this new printing medium for different series of cards, but in many cases using the same photographic view in 1939 through 1941, 1947, 1948, and 1950; no series was produced in 1949. The cards were available with a minimum gasoline purchase in Union Oil's facilities, mainly in the Midwest and the Far West.

Figure 11. 1938.

COLUMBUS CIRCLE, N. Y. . . . Famous Macy Thanks-giving Parade passing the Columbus Monument at 59th St.

Figure 12. 1939.

A less-publicized but equally early set of chrome cards was produced by Macy's department store in New York, which shows various scenes of the city. The cards are not numbered but have been reported to be a set of twelve city views, sold in a folder together with one interior view of Macy's. Figure 12 is a scene of one of Macy's giant balloons, which appear annually in the store's Thanksgiving Day Parade. The card bears a 1939 copyright.

Because of the virtually complete disregard of collectors' interests by modern postcard publishers, most chrome cards, although of exceptional quality, bear views of minimal interest, hackneyed and stereotyped, and fit mainly for sending regards to Aunt Millie. Dealers generally do not even bother to sort chrome cards into geographical locale or topic and present to the collector a shoe box to plow through, card by card. The plowing can reap a bountiful harvest because there will inevitably be some cards showing automobiles, aircraft, fashions, ships, shopping districts, and perhaps a famous person or two amid the views of the motels, the Grand Canyon, or the Rocky Mountains.

One of the few chrome sets was published by Sambo's, a nationwide chain of restaurants. This chain took as its symbol the character Little Black Sambo, the little African boy of the children's book; they transformed him into a lad living in India, complete with turban. A set of eight cards was produced, generally following the story of the African boy. The final scene of the set is illustrated in figure 13.

For all of its promotional "hype," the issuance of a numbered set of cards by Sambo's follows the tradition started way back in the prepostcard 1880s, when the Singer Sewing Machine Company came forth with a series of advertising cards showing the use of its machines in views of practically every country of the world. Collectors should feel indebted to Sambo's for offering to us the opportunity to collect modern cards by set.

Figure 13. c. 1955.

That Little Something Extra

In sorting out an accumulation of cards, a keen eye may spot two cards of a similar design, but the addition of perhaps only a line or two transforms one of the cards into something quite interesting and potentially valuable.

Figure 14. c. 1910.

Figure 15. c. 1910.

Consider the two views in figures 14 and 15. A stock view of lower Manhattan was overprinted by the makers of Lash's Bitters into a highly interesting advertising card. The picture of a Wright Brothers' Flyer adds even more to the desirability of the card.

The view of Grace Church in figure 16, although interesting in itself because of the inclusion of a trolley and a very early electric automobile parked at

Figure 16. postmarked 1929.

Figure 17. postmarked 1916.

the curb, is seen in figure 17 bearing the advertising overprint of, of all things, a bell-ringing vaudeville act.

Less obvious to a busy dealer's eye, but not to be overlooked in careful perusal by the collector, are items of advertising appearing as part of the view pictured on a card. Figure 18 extols the quality of Zeno Chewing Gum and appears as a banner over New York's Fifth Avenue.

FLAT IRON BUILDING, NEW YORK.

Figure 18. postmarked 1913.

Similarly deft retouching of the interesting but commonplace harbor scene in figure 19 places in prominence the name of the excursion boat *Zephyr*. The reverse of the card describes the daily trips of the steamer *Zephyr* to the Statue of Liberty.

Collectors coming across a card like figure 20 can congratulate themselves on discovering an added treat. They have not only a nice historic view filled with horse-drawn vehicles (in themselves highly sought-after by collectors) but the ad for a cough drop along the left border of the card.

By careful inspection of your cards, what at first might appear as a duplicate view can be found, by the insertion of an advertising legend, to be an interesting and perhaps a valuable item. The truism applies to cards produced in all eras. Inspect each card carefully for advertising.

Figure 19. c. 1920.

Figure 20. postmarked 1944.

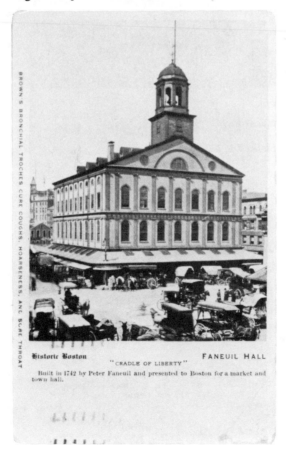

Dear Friend;— I request you not to purchase these magazines: Delineator, Designer, New Idea, nor World's Work, nor these dress patterns: Butterick, Standard, New Idea, nor Banner, as they have locked out their printers for requesting the eight-hour work day.

New York Harbor and Aquarium, Battery Park

Figure 21. c. 1910.

DEAR SIR AND BROTHER:

IF IN NEW YORK ON TUESDAY EVENING, AUGUST 11TH, 1903, A SIGHT WORTH SEEING WILL BE THE 216TH REGULAR CONVENTION OF WENDELL PHILLIPS LODGE NO. 365, K. OF P. AT THE CASTLE HALL, AND YOU WILL BE WELL REPAID BY A VISIT TO SAME FROM 8 TO 9 O'CLOCK.

FRATERNALLY YOURS,

HENRY A. ROBINSON,
KEEPER OF RECORDS AND SEAL.

EMANUEL GOLDSTEIN,
CHANCELLOR COMMANDER.

68-View of the Battery & New York Harbor, J. Koehler, N.Y

Figure 22. postmarked 1903.

Figure 23. postmarked 1907.

BATTERY PARK AND NEW CUSTOM HOUSE, N.Y.

The Platinachrome Co. N.Y.

I shall take pleasure in calling on you————————————————————————————, and hope to be favored with your business.

Representing

OVER

THE ELDRIDGE & HIGGINS CO., WHOLESALE GROCERS.

Figure 24. postmarked 1905.

Some Curious Usages

In addition to elements of advertising appearing on commonplace-view cards, collectors should be alert to cards bearing imprinted messages as in figure 21. This is an astounding call by a typographical union for a boycott of certain publications "as they have locked out their printers for requesting the eight-hour work day." A fascinating bit of social history appearing on a number of common New York City views!

Another interesting usage of a commonplace view is figure 22, a meeting announcement from the Knights of Pythias, a fraternal organization.

A visit to your town might have been the prize in a promotional campaign by a commercial organization. If so, there might have been prepared cards similar to the one in figure 23 showing your local views. This is one of a series of thirty-two issued by a firm of wholesale grocers headquartered in Findlay, Ohio. The back explains that the series was issued to publicize The Eldridge & Higgins Co.'s Great Free Excursion in August 1907. A question that is raised in the mind of a collector is, Does this item belong in a New York City or a Findlay, Ohio, geographic collection? Probably both, and in a firefighting topical collection as well, because the harbor craft on the left is a fireboat.

In an attempt to boost sales, this life insurance company issued a series of view cards in 1905 announcing a sales contest. Note in figure 24 the admonition to "Pay attention to what follows."

Foreign Languages Spoken Here

Collectors should not lose sight of the fact that most postcards were produced to be bought to send a message. With this in mind, it is not difficult to realize that many senders were either tourists or recently arrived immigrants to these shores.

Note the bilingualism on figure 25, with the insertion of the German "Gruss aus" ("greetings from") on the bottom. *Gruss aus* appearing on an American scene makes a card far more of a collectible item.

Figure 25. postmarked 1906.

A firm in Milan, Italy, named Edizione Oxford issued what appears to be a series of at least nine cards with a bilingual Italian-English text. A card with, yes again, New York's Williamsburg Bridge is shown in figure 26.

Figure 27 is a third example of a card produced for foreign consumption, but showing an American view. This card would slip by many a collector before a keen eye would notice the "U.S.A." in the text. Why would a card produced by an American company bear this legend? A glance at the back confirmed the suspicion that it was produced in England with the instruction "Affix half-penny stamp" appearing in the stamp box.

Figure 28 could lead a collector on a merry chase. Obviously a message in

Figure 26. c. 1910.

Figure 27. c. 1910.
Figure 28. c. 1898.

the Cyrillic alphabet has been overprinted on an early card produced by the Kreh Company. The language is Ukrainian—the message is an invitation to a dance. Part of it reads "Come all and bring your friends." Although the name of the hall has been obliterated on this card, comparison with another card indicates that the dance was held at Webster Hall in New York City.

Now You See It, Now You Don't

What might appear to be an exact copy of a particular view may, on closer inspection, be a prime example of what appears to be a classic case of pirating. Note the grouping of figures at the lower right on figures 29 and 30, showing Fifth Avenue in New York.

Figure 29. c. 1907.

Figure 30. c. 1907 altered view.

Figure 29 is probably the original, showing the adult couple and the two children. It was published by Success Post Card Co. (No. 2022). By eliminating some figures and altering the street traffic, it is assumed, the publisher of figure 301 (unidentified except for the letters "C.V." preceding his stock number) was able to circumvent the loosely enforced copyright laws of the early 1900s and was able to market the view as his own. Whether the poor photographer who originally snapped the photo was paid for his product and whether in fact there were any strolling pedestrians in the original view is anybody's guess.

The Camera's Eye

The vast majority of cards in a collection were mass-produced by national or even worldwide publishing firms and marketed to cater to the taste of the general population. Of particular interest are the actual photographs taken by the local photographer, or even an individual, portraying an object, event, or view of local interest. These cards can be found in the "Actual Photographs" section of a dealer's stock. The quantity and description of photographic cards are limitless. No one could even attempt to catalogue or categorize even a small portion of the thousands that have been produced over the decades. A typical narrative of the origin of this type of card would be as follows. A drugstore or other small commercial establishment would advertise that it could reproduce a photograph directly onto a photosensitive piece of cardboard stock that was purchased in quantity from, say, Eastman Kodak. The coated face of the card would bear the reproduction of the view taken directly from a negative brought in by the customer. The back of the photosensitive card would be imprinted by Kodak with the words *Post Card,* a stamp box, and a line dividing the back in half. The name of the drugstore or other merchant might be applied by rubber stamp. The view on the face could be of any topic imaginable from a one-of-a-kind view of the sender's home, family, auto, or shop to a series of cards produced in limited quantities by an enterprising merchant to publicize a town or a parade, celebration, or other local event. At the turn of the century, the reproduction of photographs in newspapers was a costly and, hence, relatively little-used process. Many local events that would now be covered by a news photographer would have been ignored were it not for the enterprising amateur photographer with his box camera who considered a view of enough interest to a friend or relative to be reproduced on a privately prepared card and mailed to him. This amateur filled the same function as the lithographic firms of the prephotography era, as for example Currier & Ives, who made their reputations by covering newsworthy events, sketching a scene and reproducing it by lithography. These firms competed with each other to get a pictorial "scoop" by being the first to portray a newsworthy event.

Consider the view in figure 31—obviously a scene of a garment manufacturer's workroom. There is no identification of the factory or the workers appearing in the view. Yet someone considered this scene of enough importance to pay for its reproduction as a postcard. Observe the bored expressions of the workers,

Figure 31. c. 1910.

who faced a ten-hour day, a six-day week, and a life of tedium, working on piles of clothing in cramped, ill-lighted, airless conditions, threatened with the ever-present danger of fire spreading through this highly flammable material. Cards such as this underline the inestimable importance of postcards in chronicling and illustrating social history.

Figure 32—as it was mailed, and therefore postmarked, and bears a message—is easier to identify. The message describes a pier fire and identifies one of the three fireboats engaged in combating it. The card bears the firm name of Merritt & Chapman Derrick & Wrecking Co. and was posted on August 26, 1910.

Many collectors ignore these photographic cards produced by obscure or even unidentifiable printers because of the difficulty in researching the view and

Figure 32. postmarked 1910.

Figure 33. postmarked 1907.   **Figure 34.** c. 1906.

the penchant on the part of the collectors for completing numbered series or sets of cards. Their collecting tastes can be satisfied by the next two actual photographic cards. Figure 33 is a multiview of New York scenes produced by M. Ettlinger & Co. (Series 4717). Figure 34 is one in a series of Chinatown views produced by one of the giants in the early postcard era, The Rotograph Co. The 1906 copyright date pertains to the photograph, not necessarily the card. Note the man's queue hanging down his back almost to his ankles! Rotograph also produced a series of multiviews numbered B1986–1990, copyrighted 1907, and bearing the legend on the back "This card is a REAL PHOTOGRAPH on bromide paper."

Photocards are very delicate and can easily be chipped and cracked—possibly another reason that collectors shun them. Protect those found in your collection—they are interesting, unique, and probably irreplaceable.

The Border

A final consideration in evaluating an accumulation of postcards is the presence of a fancy border around a view that interests you.

Publishers down through the years have delighted in getting extra sales mileage out of their stock views by reissuing them decorated with a pleasing border. Not to be confused with the products of the white bordered era, during which publishers stinted on the use of inks, the decorative borders serve to enhance and complement the view portrayed. Note the pleasing park scene (figure 35) showing a bridle path in New York's Central Park surrounded by a simulated wood border, produced by a printer who is unfortunately unidentified. The wood adds to the rustic quality of the view.

Similarly, figure 36 shows a street scene of Chinatown enhanced by the inclusion of bamboo stalks as a border on this linen card (No. K 6369) produced by the Manhattan Post Card Publishing Company.

For a fledgling collector, the best advice is to discard no card unless it is an exact duplicate. Even the slightest variation on the face or back of a card might be of significance and importance in developing the accumulation of cards you have gathered into a thoroughly researched and categorized collection.

Figure 35. postmarked 1910.

Figure 36. c. 1940.

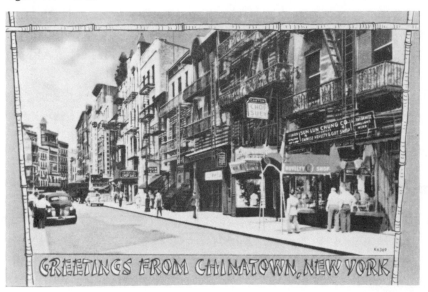

3

The Flip Side

There is one feature common to every picture postcard ever produced: indications on the back of the card that it was printed to be used to deliver a message through the mail. Without this back, the picture on the front, however beautiful and interesting, remains just that, a picture and not a part of a postcard collection.

Take any ordinary card like figure 37 distributed by a mountain resort. The back is divided in half, forming a section on the left for a message and one on the right for the address of the recipient. A "stamp box" appears in the upper right corner of the card. A description of the view on the front of the card generally appears on the "message side"—in this case, the description is a small advertisement for the resort. The *K* in the diamond symbol in the lower left corner is the "logo" or trademark of the company that printed this card, the Koppel Company.

Serving as the line dividing the back of this card is what is known in the hobby as the credit line, where the distributor or publisher of the card takes credit for the job it has done in selecting the photograph reproduced on the front, designing the layout, etc. The final item of interest is the number appearing on the back; in this case, it's merely a stock number put there by the printer, Koppel, for inventory purposes. The publisher might come back with another order, "Run off 10,000 more copies of number 140774."

The form of the back of modern cards is taken for granted by the fledgling collector. There is, however, a fascinating story behind the development of the back of cards. From a study of the backs, the history of the evolution of postcards can be traced.

Figure 37. c. 1970.

It's time you discovered
Kutsher's Country Club
Monticello, New York

A "SUPERCHROME" Color Product by Bill Bard Associates Inc., Monticello, N.Y.

POST CARD
Address

PLACE
STAMP
HERE

140774

The Evolution of the "Back"

It took an act of Congress, with attendant lobbying by publishers and printers and political pressure by the general public, to break the monopoly held by the U.S. Post Office (USPO) over the production and use of messages in card form being sent through the mails. The USPO had its postal cards for sale at the post office for one cent. It also had its two-cent stamps available to be used to mail letters. It was not about to allow privately produced cards to be mailed at a rate of less than two cents. The public, particularly tourists, balked at the premium price they had to pay to send a short message to Aunt Tillie, and Congress finally acted. The so-called Private Mailing Card Act of May 19, 1898, allowed the general public to buy a privately produced card with a view they particularly enjoyed and to mail it at the one-cent rate rather than the two-cent letter rate previously charged by the USPO.

Figure 38 is a good example of the transitional period in which privately produced cards were accorded the one-cent postage rate.

You will note that the stamp box instructs the sender to affix a two-cent stamp. By the use of what appears to be a rubber stamp, this card was overprinted with an "authorization" line indicating that Congress allowed this card to be mailed at the one-cent rate of the USPO postal cards. (The actual date of the act was May 19, 1898, as stated, rather than the May 9 imprinted on this card.)

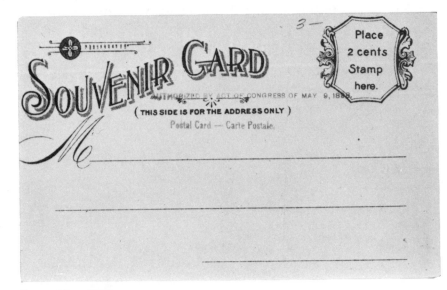

Figure 38. c. 1897.

The USPO was reluctant to have its product, the postal card, identified with the privately produced cards. It therefore required publishers to identify their products with a description dissimilar to the USPO's wording. The publishers selected the term *private mailing card* to distinguish their privately produced cards, as in figure 39.

Note that these private mailing cards, known to the hobbyists as PMCs,

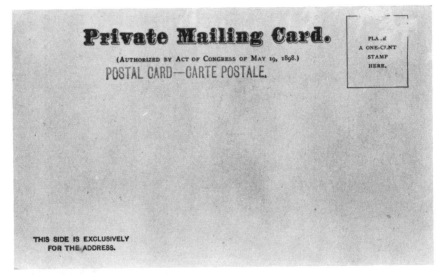

Figure 39. c. 1900.

could be mailed for the one-cent rate, bore the authorization line, and could be written on only on the front of the card—the back being used "exclusively for the address." Many PMCs bear the bilingual inscription indicating that the card was eligible to enter the international mail system operated under the provisions of the Universal Postal Union. This card was overprinted by rubber stamps. Other PMCs had the bilingual legend printed on the back.

The act of Congress became effective on July 1, 1898. It stipulated that PMCs would have to approximate government postal cards in size, quality, and weight. To this day, most postcards have followed these general guidelines. There was a further relaxation of postal regulations in December 1901, when by Post Office Order No. 1447 the term *post card* could be used rather than the lengthier PMC legend and authorization line. Thus the first era of the postcard, the PMC era, lasted from July 1, 1898, to December 24, 1901, although PMCs could and still can, with the proper postage, be used in the mails.

The USPO remained firm in its insistence that no message appear on the back of a postcard. But faced with increasing public resistance to being forced to cram messages, advertisements, and return addresses on the fronts of cards, the USPO further relaxed its regulations by allowing the sender's name and address to appear on the back of the postcard without charging the two-cent letter rate.

Here are two examples of the way publishers gave recognition to this development. Figure 40, an odd-sized card, tells the story under its "rates of postage." Figure 41 bears the warning, "No other writing!"

The final stage in the evolution of postcard backs started on March 1, 1907, when the USPO allowed a written message to share the back with the address. One can imagine the wringing of hands of postmasters and clerks in their distress over the revenue supposedly lost to patrons who preferred to send a note via postcard rather than a two-cent letter. What they could not envision were the millions upon millions of cards emanating from resorts, vacation spots, huge cities,

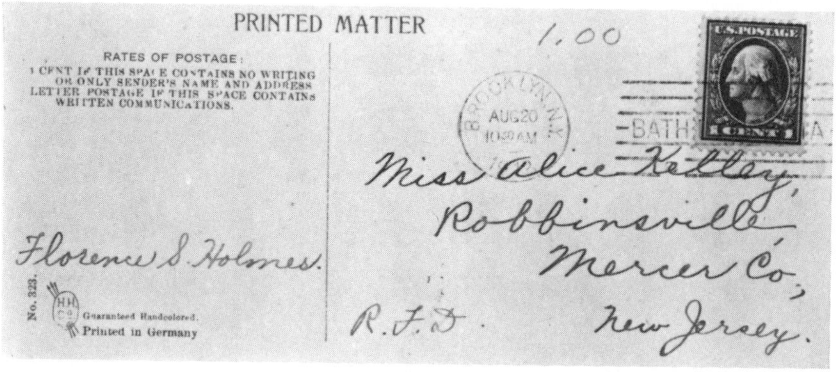

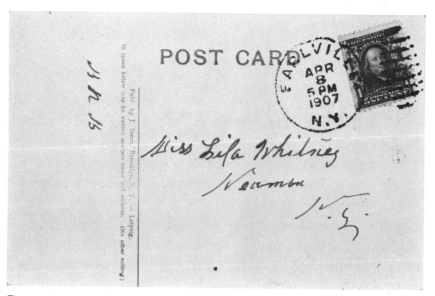

Figure 40. postmarked 1912.

Figure 41. postmarked 1907.

and tiny hamlets and the advertising and promotional material from practically every type of commercial establishment, each bearing its message and, if mailed, its green one-cent stamp.

The early divided backs looked like figure 42, with the instructions that the left could be used for correspondence after March 1, 1907.

Advertising

The floodgates were now open for postcards to be used for messages, both printed and handwritten, that had hitherto been confined to the front of the card. There follow just a few of the thousands of advertising messages to be found among a dealer's wares that he and other casual collectors might have overlooked in their emphasis on what appears on the picture side of the card.

In figures 43 and 44 the makers of Castle Coffee chose stock views of New York's Castle Clinton to carry these ads, which were printed on the back.

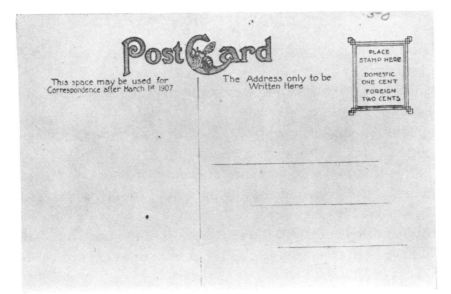

Figure 42. c. 1907.

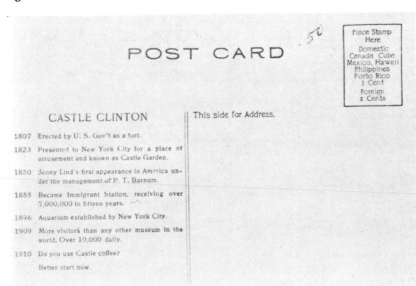

Figure 43. c. 1910.

Figure 44. postmarked 1913.

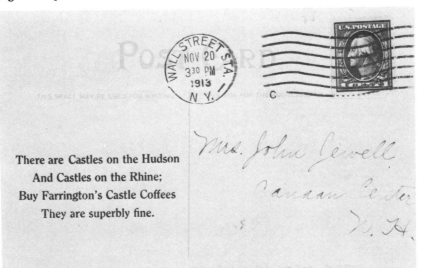

In figure 45 a menu appears on the card—note the price and the bill of fare, with orchestra music to boot!

A bank chose the postcard as a medium to publish its financial statement, as in figure 46.

A commercial establishment acknowledged an order with figure 47 addressed to a customer.

Of particular interest to postcard collectors are ads for postcards themselves. Here are a few overprinted by the publishers on their own cards.

Figure 48, used by the excellent Rotograph Co., gives a concise review of the production of cards in the 1900s. Note the cost of the card, one-half cent. The cards would have been sold to the public at at least one cent apiece.

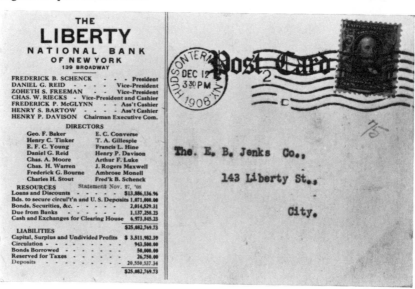

Figure 45. postmarked 1909.

Figure 46. postmarked 1908.

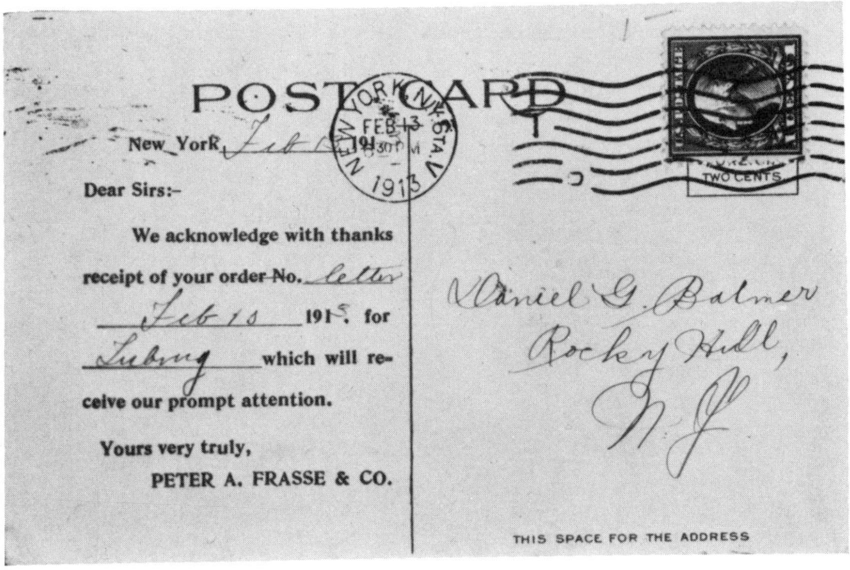

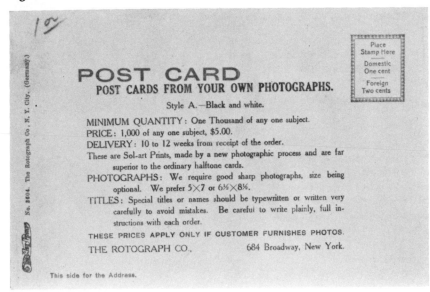

Figure 47. postmarked 1913.

Figure 48. c. 1905.

Figures 49 and 50 are two examples of ads from modern publishers. Lumitone appears to have specialized in hotels and other public buildings. Their customers number in the thousands. The price of a card, like everything else, has escalated in fifty years or so. Colorart advertised cards priced from 1.3¢ to 3.2¢ apiece.

In figure 51, an enterprising retailer rubber-stamped a quantity of cards advertising the location of his shop.

Not all advertising messages appeared in printed form. Many concerns used script to disguise their ad as a handwritten message. It's easy to spot this ruse on a card never mailed, as illustrated in figure 52 advertising a movie and vaudeville theatre. Note the prices and the description of a movie as a "photo play," and the unfortunate misspelling of *vaudeville*.

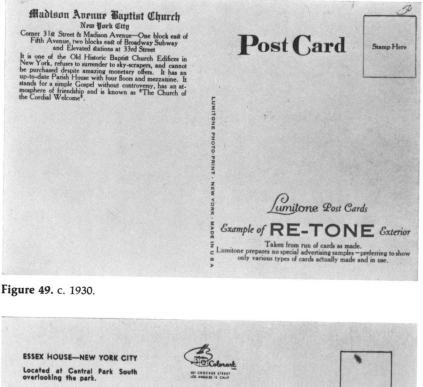

Madison Avenue Baptist Church
New York City
Corner 31st Street & Madison Avenue—One block east of
Fifth Avenue, two blocks east of Broadway Subway
and Elevated stations at 33rd Street

It is one of the Old Historic Baptist Church Edifices in
New York, refuses to surrender to sky-scrapers, and cannot
be purchased despite amazing monetary offers. It has an
up-to-date Parish House with four floors and mezzanine. It
stands for a simple Gospel without controversy, has an at-
mosphere of friendship and is known as "The Church of
the Cordial Welcome".

Post Card

Stamp Here

LUMITONE PHOTO-PRINT · NEW YORK · MADE IN U.S.A.

Lumitone Post Cards

Example of **RE-TONE** *Exterior*

Taken from run of cards as made.
Lumitone prepares no special advertising samples — preferring to show
only various types of cards actually made and in use.

Figure 49. c. 1930.

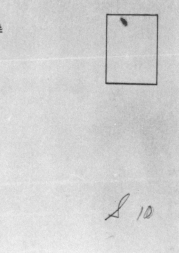

ESSEX HOUSE—NEW YORK CITY

Located at Central Park South
overlooking the park.

Colorart
387 CROCKER STREET
LOS ANGELES 13 CALIF

NATURAL COLOR POST CARDS

WILL POPULARIZE YOUR HOTEL

Let your guests send full color post cards
of your accommodations to their friends
far and near. Natural color post cards are
your most effective and inexpensive method
of advertising. Cards are priced as low as
1½ cents each or you may have 3000 cards
for only $95.00.

For details write to

COLORART INC. of NEW YORK

475 FIFTH AVENUE
NEW YORK, N. Y.

Telephone MUrray Hill 3-3421

COLORART, INC. OF NEW YORK · 225 BROADWAY, NEW YORK 13, NEW YORK

Figure 50. c. 1950.

Figure 51. c. 1905.

POST CARD

THIS SIDE IS FOR THE ADDRESS ONLY.

Place
Stamp Here

Domestic
One cent

Foreign
Two cents

Nº 515 UNITED ART PUBLISHING Cº (PRINTED IN GERMANY)

LESLIE E. CARL,
The Deposit Jeweler
IS SELLING POST CARDS
NEAR THE MERRY-GO-ROUND.
CARDS LIKE THIS 1 CENT EACH.

In figure 57 a professional society used the Hudson-Fulton Celebration as if it were incidental to its own convention at the same time in 1909. It is hoped that the recipient dropped in to the convention after watching the two-week-long celebration held up and down the Hudson River.

As noted previously, the use of postage other than a postage stamp to mail a card is relatively rare but by no means an indication of increased value of the card. The inclusion of cards imprinted on the back with a sender's bulk-rate permit number is just another element in a good postcard collection. Figure 58 bears the imprint of a seed supplier and was sent to a woman in Saskatchewan, Canada. The addressee, Mrs. Lund, ultimately founded the town of Mozart, Saskatchewan. (Articles by the eminent writer-philatelist George T. Guzzio on the postal history of Mozart make interesting reading.)

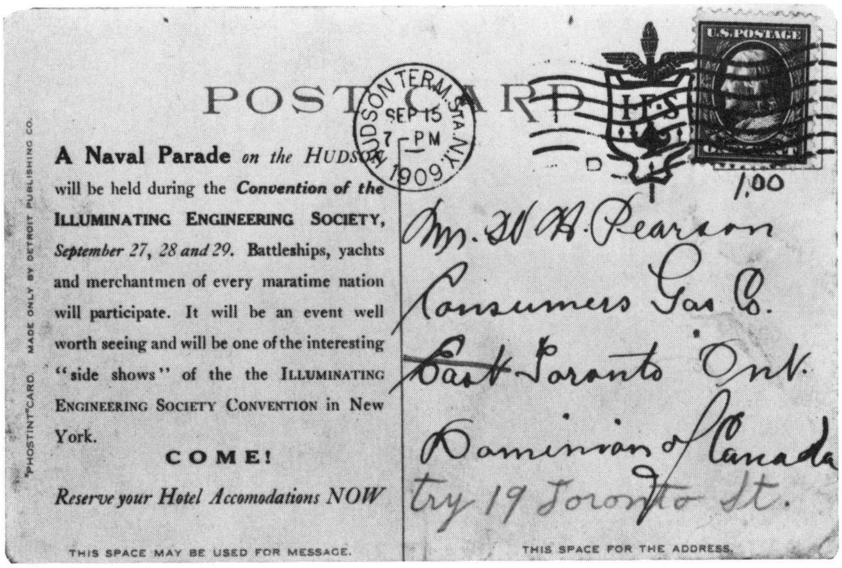

Figure 57. postmarked 1909.

Figure 58. 1910.

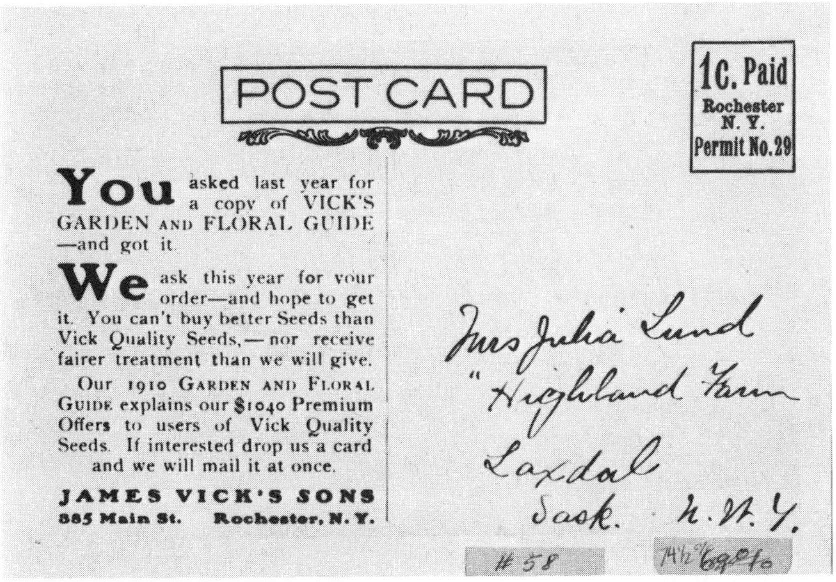

Later uses of permit imprints on postcards are the two items in figures 59 and 60. Figure 59 is an invitation to a first-day-of-issue ceremony of a postage stamp at an educational institution. The organization of the famous evangelist Billy Graham issued figure 60 publicizing a rally. Note the simulated handwriting and signature on the message side.

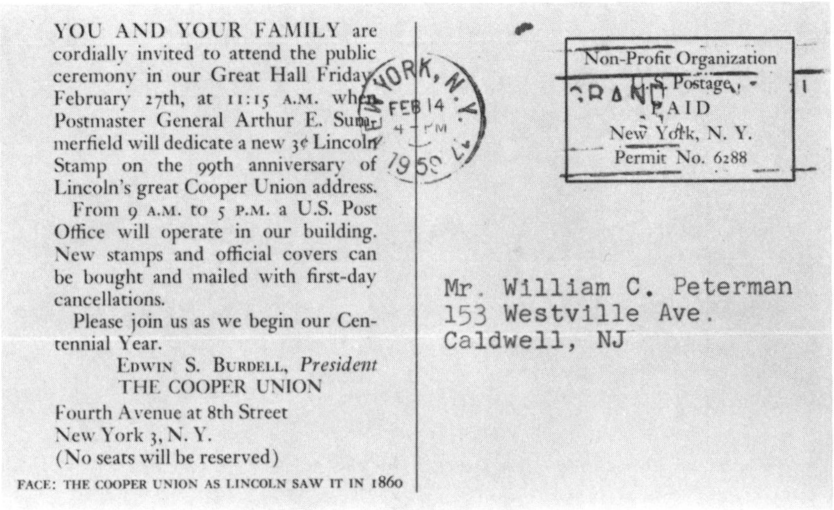

YOU AND YOUR FAMILY are cordially invited to attend the public ceremony in our Great Hall Friday, February 27th, at 11:15 A.M. when Postmaster General Arthur E. Summerfield will dedicate a new 3¢ Lincoln Stamp on the 99th anniversary of Lincoln's great Cooper Union address.

From 9 A.M. to 5 P.M. a U.S. Post Office will operate in our building. New stamps and official covers can be bought and mailed with first-day cancellations.

Please join us as we begin our Centennial Year.

EDWIN S. BURDELL, *President*
THE COOPER UNION
Fourth Avenue at 8th Street
New York 3, N. Y.
(No seats will be reserved)

FACE: THE COOPER UNION AS LINCOLN SAW IT IN 1860

NEW YORK, N.Y. FEB 14 4 PM 1959

Non-Profit Organization
U.S. Postage
PAID
New York, N. Y.
Permit No. 6288

Mr. William C. Peterman
153 Westville Ave.
Caldwell, NJ

Figure 59. postmarked 1959.

Figure 60. c. 1960.

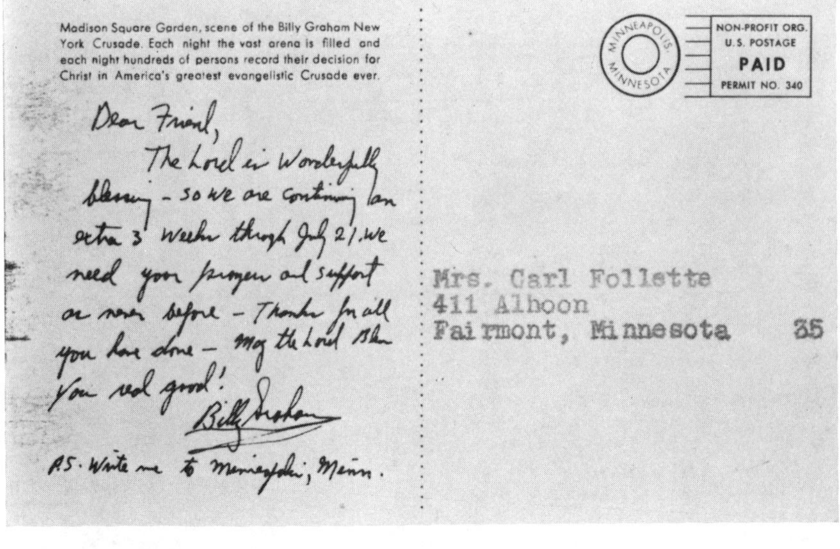

Madison Square Garden, scene of the Billy Graham New York Crusade. Each night the vast arena is filled and each night hundreds of persons record their decision for Christ in America's greatest evangelistic Crusade ever.

Dear Friend,
The Lord is wonderfully blessing - so we are continuing an extra 3 weeks through July 21. We need your prayers and support as never before - Thanks for all you have done - May the Lord bless you real good!
Billy Graham
P.S. Write me to Minneapolis, Minn.

MINNEAPOLIS MINNESOTA

NON-PROFIT ORG.
U.S. POSTAGE
PAID
PERMIT NO. 340

Mrs. Carl Follette
411 Alhoon
Fairmont, Minnesota 35

Curious Usages

Figure 61, showing a troopship passing the Statue of Liberty on the front, was published by the YMCA and given free to returning World War I doughboys. It was used by the soldier to notify his folks of his arrival in the United States. Note that postage was free if the card was mailed "on boat or dock." The two-cent rate noted in the stamp box reflects a one-cent surcharge imposed on all classes of mail during and shortly after World War I, the proceeds to be used in the war effort. A variety of this card exists, with a smaller YMCA logo.

A particularly virulent piece of propaganda shows up on the face of figure 62, with "Washington, D.C." already printed on the address side—and instructions in the stamp box. The front of the card shows Uncle Sam as the Pied Piper tooting a horn inscribed "Immigration Laws," leading out of Europe rats labeled "thief," "assassin," "incendiary," and "murderer" and carrying in their mouths knives, torches, guns, and papers marked "Black Hand." Figures in European national costumes labeled "Italy," "Russia," "Hungary," and so on cheer the exodus from their shores of these social undesirables to America. The object of this satirical cartoon, identified as "From Puck," is of course an appeal for stricter immigration laws. The individual or group sponsoring this card is unidentified.

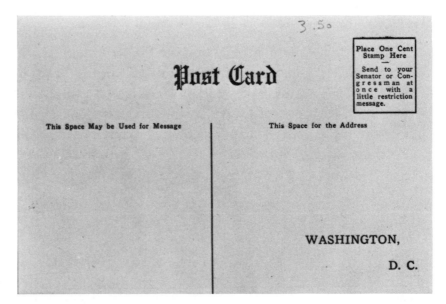

Figure 62. c. 1910.

Figure 63, showing a photo of the United Nations Secretariat Building, bears the legend, "The House That Hiss Built." The flip side of this card appears below. The Hiss, of course, is Alger Hiss, a former State Department official who was found guilty of perjury in a celebrated and controversial espionage trial in the 1950s.

An ingenious card-addressing service was advertised on figure 64. How could he have made any money, selling this service for 2.5¢ per card?

A civic organization publicized the availability of travel literature in figure 65, sent to Chambers of Commerce throughout the country.

In figure 66, a thoughtful printer corrected data appearing on the front of this card, noting that "plans changed" in the dimensions of the building pictured.

Figure 63. 1962.

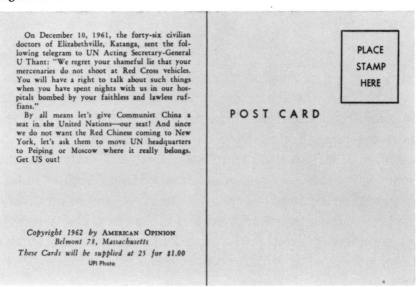

Figure 64. postmarked 1908.

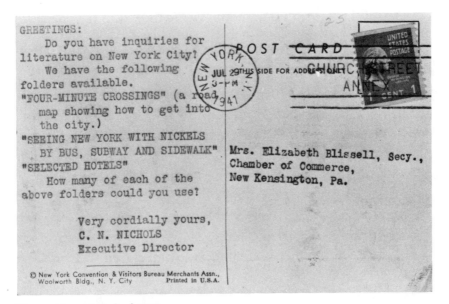

Figure 65. postmarked 1941.

Figure 66. postmarked 1908.

The Message

It is a rare collector who will take the time to read the written message on the cards he has acquired. Of course, 99.9 percent are as bland and colorless as that appearing in figure 66. Occasionally, at his leisure, the collector will browse through his cards and co   cross a few items that can take their place in social history.

Traveling in the grand manner is described on a card dated in January 1916 and sent from New York to Everett, Massachusetts:

> Train ½ hr. late and boat did not come for another ½ hr. I was cold waiting for boat. Music on board was fine but only heard 3 pieces. Had inside stateroom and in morning went to Child's Rest. on Fulton St. We are stopping at Hotel Theresa.

On a card picturing a college for women, postmarked in August 1928:

> This is one of the women's dormitories where they keep the young, tender plants under 23. Having passed that stage and become a member of the old hen class, I am not eligible, but am living at (address). Mail is very nice when received at this address.

Some youngsters devised their own code, as shown in figure 67. The recipient decoded it, to our benefit. Fortunately no state secrets were disclosed to "His Nibs."

Another message on a card, postmarked March 7, 1917, reads: "Down here for a few days. Saw the return of the 69th Reg." The "Fighting 69th" marched off to war in France just a few months after their March 1917 return from the Mexican border.

A companion piece to the above message is that on a card dated April 6, 1917: "I was down to the waterfront today to see all the war aeroplanes and balloons." April 6, 1917—the day the United States declared war on Germany.

Figure 67. postmarked 1910.

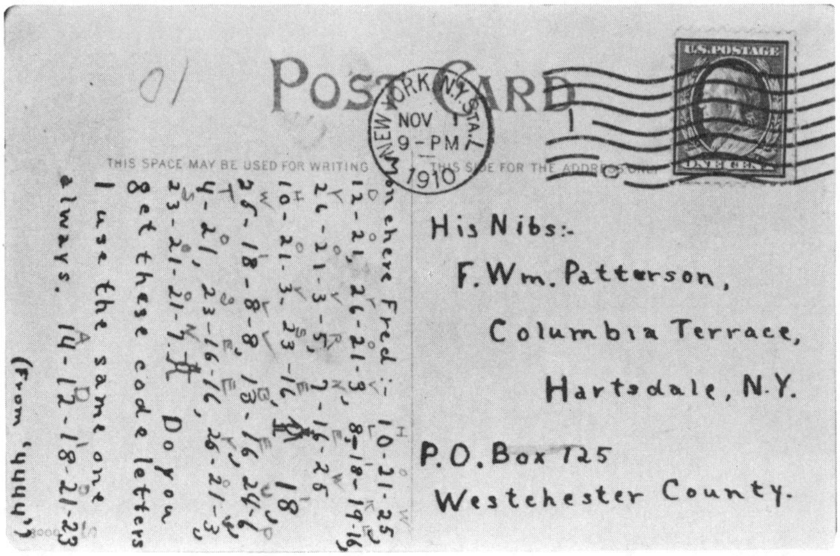

A message that, when read, makes the reader feel like an eavesdropper, is one like this: "He is not working. Things are in pretty bad shape here, getting worse all the time." The date on this pathetic message—October 31, 1933, the depths of the Depression.

The Philatelic Connection

As you browse through a dealer's box, you might notice customers completely ignoring the fronts of the cards and carefully inspecting each back. Invariably they are stamp collectors looking for interesting stamps and postmarks. An oft-repeated adage is "Look for stamps at a postcard show—look for cards at a stamp show."

There is truth in this adage as exemplified by figure 68. Putting on your stamp collector's hat, you can identify the U.S. stamp as being the two-cent value of the Trans-Mississippi set issued June 10, 1898. The card was addressed to Basel, Switzerland, with insufficient postage and was therefore "T-dued" at the Basel post office; that is, a rubber-stamp marking was applied to the card indicating that fifteen centimes was due from the addressee. An additional fifteen centimes was charged as a penalty for the postage due. Two postage-due stamps of Switzerland, totaling the thirty centimes owed, were therefore affixed as an indication that the amount was to be collected from the addressee. Whether Mrs. E. Frey was sufficiently interested in the card and message to shell out this cash is a matter of conjecture. Also a matter of conjecture is the reason for the postage due in the first place. As U.S. citizens were allowed to send postcards through the mail at the one-cent domestic, two-cent foreign rates by July 1, 1898, this card should have gone through for the two-cent postage affixed. Perhaps the Basel post office had not been informed of the acceptance of privately produced cards in the interna-

Figure 68. postmarked 1898.

tional mail, or perhaps private mailing cards were not accepted by the Universal Postal Union until sometime after the date that this card was mailed. An interesting question for a postal historian.

The final illustration of the importance of inspecting "the flip side" is figure 69—the back of an extremely commonplace, mediocre, and really ugly linen card showing New York's Herald Square. This card was mailed from Tibet with a stamp of India (the country that handled Tibet's external affairs). The postmark date unfortunately is indistinct; the stamp, however, was issued August 15, 1949, indicating that the card was posted no earlier than that date. Why a common New York view card was transported halfway around the world, mailed to Rockford, Illinois, and wound up in a postcard dealer's box priced at ten cents is anybody's guess.

Figure 69. c. 1959.

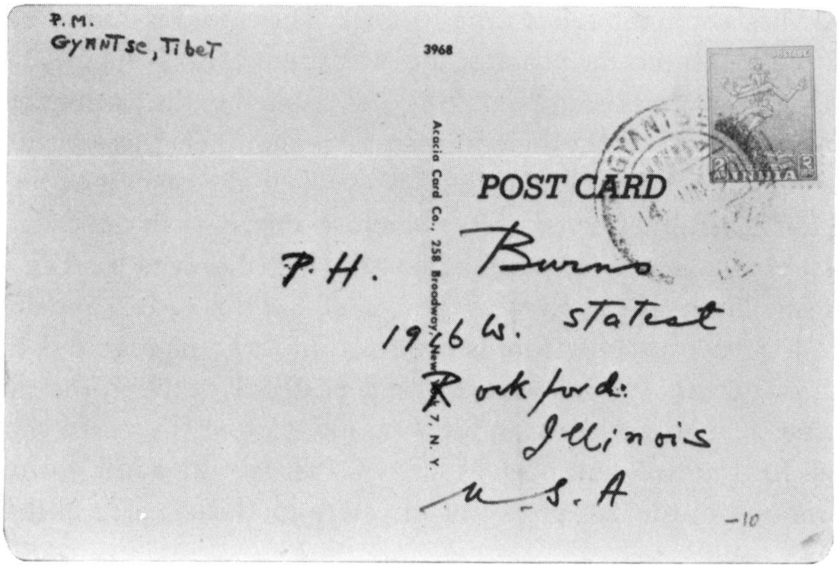

On inspecting the illustrations in this chapter outlining the importance of the backs of cards, you will note light indications of prices. These were applied by dealers selling the cards that were purchased during the mid-1970s. They should not be construed to be current prices. Prices vary by dealer, location, condition, and the subject appearing on the front of the card. No writer can gauge with any accuracy the monetary value of a particular card. One of the few mentions of price that will be found in these pages appears in chapter 8, "Exotica, Not Erotica."

4

The Joys of Research

Quite often, the first question asked of a postcard collector is "How many cards do you have?" The answer would be, 10,000, twenty shoe boxes, etc. A more valid question would be "What do you collect? In what do you specialize?" Playing the numbers game can be meaningless if the collector fails to take the time to find out the story behind the cards in his collection. Using the trick of the newspaper reporter, a serious collector should try to answer the basic questions: who, what, when, where, and how.

Who

Every card was published by a publishing firm, whether it be the local druggist, who contracted with a photographer to snap a series of local views to be reproduced on postcard stock for sale in his shop, or the giant commercial publishers of the past—Strauss, Livingston, Tuck, Mitchell, Detroit Publishing, Rotograph—or the modern Mike Roberts. Most of these publishers have identified themselves on their cards, either by name or by their logos, or trademarks. Often their products are sequentially numbered, making it easier to maintain a checklist of cards issued by a particular publisher. Many collectors maintain collections of all cards of a particular publisher, analogous to a stamp collector's specializing in collecting all the stamps issued by Switzerland, Ireland, or Israel. Much harder, but equally interesting, would be the collecting of photographs of individual photographers that appear on cards. Most times, the photographer is *not* identified on a card, and researching in this area would entail hours of joyful browsing through the photography section of a large library.

Literature on the older publishing houses exists, with new entrants to the field being researched through the postcard-club publications. Items currently available are listed in the Bibliography. A few are listed below:

Andrews, Barbara. *A Directory of Postcards, Publishers and Trademarks, 1975*

Carver, Sally. *The American Postcard Guide to Tuck, 1976*

Jenkinson, David H. *Edward Mitchell: A Checklist of the D and T Postcards, 1977*

Lackey, Bernard B. *Handbook for Issues of Edward H. Mitchell, Publisher, 1975*

Papell, Ben, and Lorne, James. *Detroit Publishing Co. Collector's Guide, 1975*

Illustrations of cards produced by these major houses are to be found throughout this book, with number references if available.

There are few postcard collections that do not contain at least one card from the publishing house of Raphael Tuck & Sons. An English firm, it introduced collecting by sets to the general European market in the 1890s and was equipped to inundate the American market with quality material when the floodgates were opened by an act of Congress in 1898. The Tuck firm appears to be the *ne plus ultra* in satisfying, indeed creating, the desire to collect cards, particularly by set or series. An unfortunate comparison would be between the almost-monthly emissions of Tuck and the stamp-issuing policies of the "sand-dune countries" of philatelic infamy, which produced items purely for purchase by gullible stamp collectors with no regard for postal purposes.

Tuck, however, made no bones about their postcards. They were produced solely for the benefit of collectors—to be put away for the enjoyment of the viewer—and their sets cover the broad spectrum of popular topics and views.

Figure 70. c. 1900.

Figure 70 is the back of a card published for sale in the United States by Raphael Tuck & Sons. The company's logo, the easel and palette, appear in the stamp box. The device to the left is, of course, the arms of the Crown of England. As Tuck's products were purchased by the royal household, the company was allowed to imprint the arms on its products, together with the announcement of their being "Art Publishers to Their Majesties the King & Queen." One disconcerting aspect of collecting Tuck cards is the firm's numbering system. Figure 70 notes "Postcard Series 1014." This signifies not that this individual card was assigned number 1014 but that it is one of a series of like views—in this case New York's "Little Italy"—issued under this series number. Tuck's city series generally consisted of six view cards, but it could span over a dozen cards. Its set of state capitols consists of forty-five cards, all reproductions of oil paintings issued under the trade name Oilette. Many of the Oilette cards were painted by Tuck's artist, Charles F. Flower, who, through the imaginative insertion of buses and trolleys into his paintings, made street scenes come alive. An Oilette series card signed by Flower appears in figure 71, from series No. 2057, "Central Park."

Figure 71. postmarked 1906.

An example of Tuck's "plate-marked" set appears in figure 72, with the publisher using the prefix *P* before its usual four-digit number. A February 1908 advertisement for this plate-marked series reads, "Each little subject is set in a plate-marked center on a specially prepared stout card, with white margin imprinted with title. . . ." Quotations also appear on cards with views other than of New York.

For quality of black-and-white views, few publishers are the peers of The Rotograph Co. of New York City, which bought out a venerable local New York City firm—National Art Views—in 1904. Primarily a producer of view cards, Rotograph can be credited with securing the patent for one of the most interesting of exotic cards (see chapter 8), the novelty item named "The Album Post Card." The

Figure 72. c. 1908.

company produced its share of signed artists and photocards "printed on bromide paper." Examples of the technical precision of Rotograph's photographers appear in the section of this chapter discussing researching the subject of the card.

Rotograph used a logical sequential numbering system with an alphabetical prefix indicating a series, the letter *A* indicating black-and-white; *G*, the same view in soft color; *S*, sepia; *D*, blue Delft, etc. The company produced double-paneled cards, to be folded over for mailing, designated *PE*, *PG*, and *PH* for colored views and *PA* for black-and-white.

Figure 73 is an advertising card for a newspaper. It bears virtually no resemblance to the usual Rotograph style, yet it was published by the company (No. 62906), probably under contract to its newspaper customer. More interesting is the notation on the back that the card was printed in Great Britain. Virtually all Rotograph cards were printed in Germany, as were the cards of National Art Views. It was postmarked February 19, 1908.

A delicately colored series of scenes of Japan was produced by Rotograph. One in the series is figure 74.

The Detroit Publishing Company is considered the paragon of the early publishers in the production of colored cards through lithography. Although individual companies' processes were jealously guarded, the general process of color lithography is known to require the use of a different slab of stone for each color used—limestone from Bavaria was considered the best. Aloys Senefelder of Ger-

Figure 73. postmarked 1908.

Figure 74. postmarked 1907.

many developed this process in 1796, and it was used extensively for printing by such firms as Currier & Ives throughout the nineteenth century.

Detroit Publishing was an affiliate of Detroit Photographic Company, a company supplying photographs for books and magazines and for commercial uses. A subsidiary company acquired the American rights to a Swiss printing process called Photocrom, and the Photocrom Company was formed to market colored postcards subsequent to the Private Mailing Card Act of 1898. By 1901 the name *Photocrom* had been dropped in favor of the name *Detroit Photographic Company*, and cards were issued in a series numbered 5000 and up. Detroit's range of views, many taken by landscape photographer William Henry Jackson, who joined the firm in 1898, are literally of hemispheric appeal, with representations of Canada, Mexico, and the West Indies. A typical card with a human interest appeal is figure 75—a mundane subject tenderly depicted.

Figure 75. c. 1905.

Detroit's unexcelled printing process cost money—more money than the public was willing to pay when other publishers' cards could be had for ten cents a dozen. Detroit went into receivership in 1924 but continued to publish under court direction until 1932. The last card, printed under its trade name "Phostint" appeared in 1931, depicting the Waldorf-Astoria Hotel, which opened in that year. Figure 76 shows an artist's conception of the new hotel.

Detroit benefited immeasurably, particularly in its declining days, by its contracts with the Fred Harvey chain of western restaurants. Figure 77 is an obvious Detroit card—"The Hopi House, Grand Canyon of Arizona"—produced on contract from Fred Harvey, with no indication on front or back that the card was published by Detroit. Figure 78 shows the back of another contract card, the Fred Harvey logo, and Detroit's "Phostint" trademark.

Detroit Publishing was forced into liquidation in 1932, a victim of its own excellence. The quality of its product will never be duplicated.

Edward H. Mitchell of San Francisco, like Detroit Publishing, concentrated on views and had its own printing plant. Mitchell began producing cards after the 1898 Act. Though considered a local—that is, West Coast—publisher, his "exaggerations" series of cards (for example, figure 79) has a general appeal. Many cards

Figure 76. 1931.

Figure 77. c. 1905.

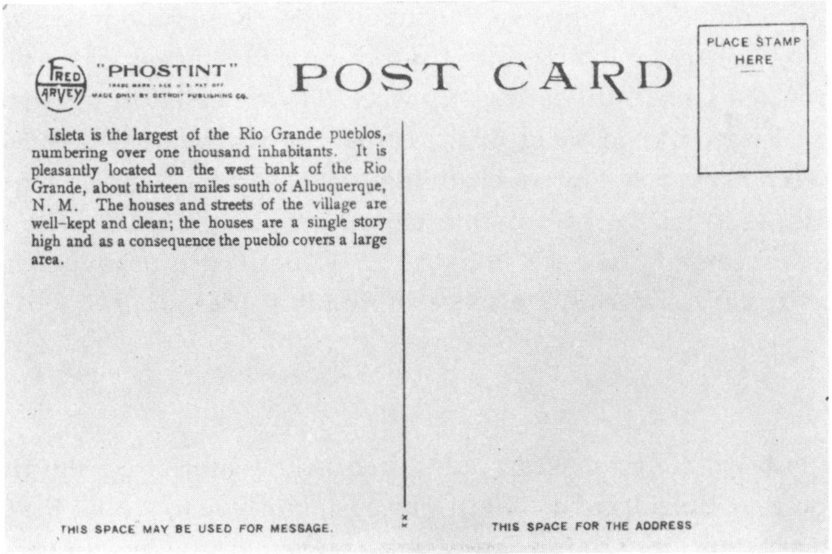

Figure 78. c. 1920.

Figure 79. postmarked 1909.

using the same flatcar (Southern Pacific 48726), but picturing giant fruit, vegetables, and other produce, were printed by Mitchell. This card was postmarked in June 1909.

In-depth studies of Mitchell cards elicit incidents of whimsy (one hesitates to say fraud) where cards with the exact same view are identified as completely different locations: a card picturing a eucalyptus tree being reissued with oranges growing on the tree; a huge American flag on the rather diminutive custom house in Monterey, California; and even a card assigned the number 27½. Because of the blatant inconsistencies, the collecting of Mitchell cards seems to be a "fun" specialization.

Of the modern publishers, there appears to be only one major firm that has any awareness of collectors' interests. Mike Roberts of Berkeley, California, spans the era of the modern "chrome" cards from its origins in the series of cards produced for the Union Oil Company starting in 1939. Roberts himself was a commercial photographer employing color Kodachrome film. Many of his photos were reproduced in the Union Oil series. His work has appeared in other publishers' efforts, as evidenced by the backs of the cards reproduced in figures 80–83.

The Fred Harvey restaurant chain (figure 81) contracted for a series of cards from Roberts, as it had decades before from Detroit Publishing. The firm's distinctive logo appears on the back in figure 82. Roberts also produced figure 83, a continental-size card picturing the space shuttle in its design.

What

If a postcard collector is not interested in the subject on the front of the card, he should be considered a collector of postal history to whom the stamp and cancellation are most important. The designs—whether drawings, cartoons, litho-

Figure 80. c. 1943.

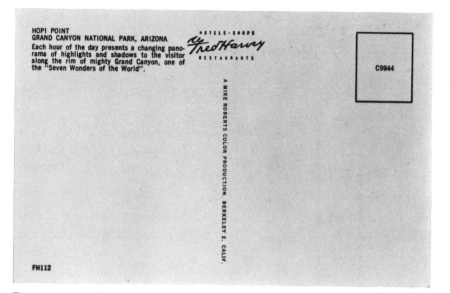

HOPI POINT
GRAND CANYON NATIONAL PARK, ARIZONA
Each hour of the day presents a changing pano-
rama of highlights and shadows to the visitor
along the rim of mighty Grand Canyon, one of
the "Seven Wonders of the World".

A MIKE ROBERTS COLOR PRODUCTION, BERKELEY 2, CALIF.

C9944

FH112

Figure 81. c. 1950.

C552 DOWNSTREAM FACE OF BOUL-
DER DAM AS SEEN FROM RIVER
LEVEL.

Color Card

REPRODUCTION FROM MIKE ROBERTS KODACHROME DISTRIBUTED
BY DESERT SOUVENIR SUPPLY, BOULDER CITY, NEVADA

Address

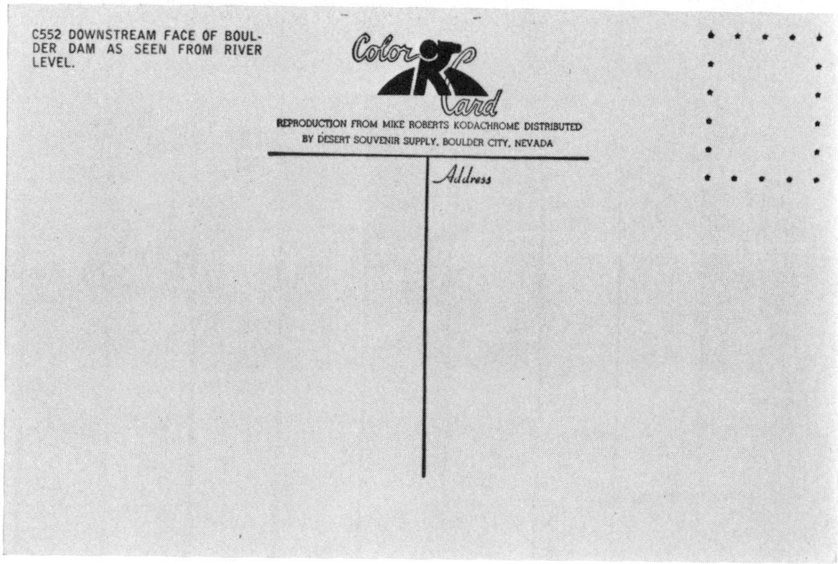

Figure 82. c. 1950.

Figure 83. c. 1977.

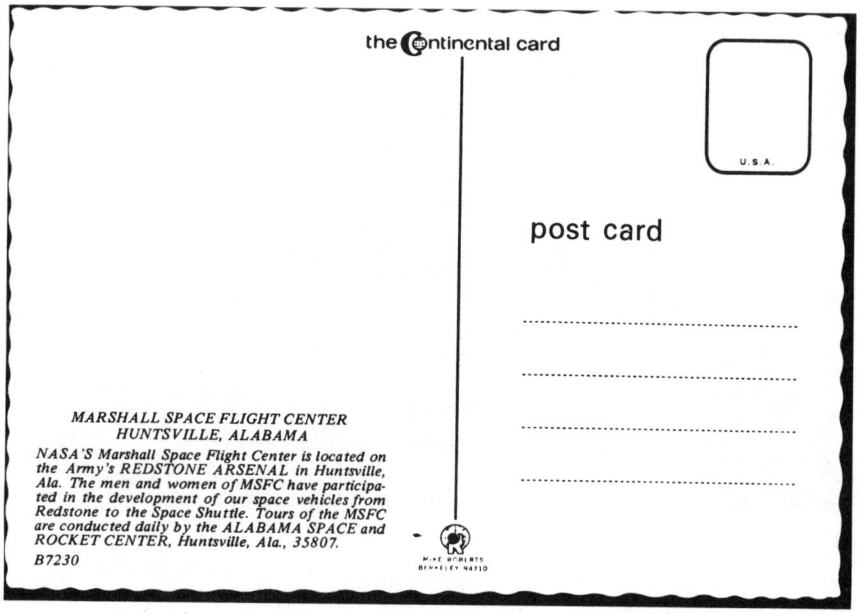

the **Continental** card

U.S.A.

post card

MARSHALL SPACE FLIGHT CENTER
HUNTSVILLE, ALABAMA

*NASA'S Marshall Space Flight Center is located on
the Army's REDSTONE ARSENAL in Huntsville,
Ala. The men and women of MSFC have participated in the development of our space vehicles from
Redstone to the Space Shuttle. Tours of the MSFC
are conducted daily by the ALABAMA SPACE and
ROCKET CENTER, Huntsville, Ala., 35807.*

B7230

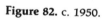

MIKE ROBERTS
BERKELEY 94710

graphs, or photographs—appearing on picture postcards are what deltiology is all about.

The obvious beginning for researching the picture is the card itself. The earlier publishers usually identified views similarly to the illustration in figure 84. This card, produced by H. Hagemeister Co. and mailed in 1909, made the search for the names of these buildings relatively easy. Consulting a New York guidebook of around 1910 will give you the street location, the architects, years of completion, and the dimensions of the buildings pictured. This information will in turn inspire you to find cards showing these buildings separately. Knowing their locations, you will want to visit the sites to see if they still exist or if they have been torn down and replaced.

Figure 84. postmarked 1909.

Figure 85. c. 1970.

You will then be able to identify the buildings in a modern view like figure 85. Note the enormous change in this location, with only the now-diminutive West Street Building appearing in prominence on the modern card, published by the Manhattan Post Card Pub. Co. Inspection of the modern card will in turn prompt you to research the World Trade Center towers and the other buildings in this view.

Similar techniques will yield information on the building appearing on the Rotograph card in figure 86. But what of the names appearing on the pennant? By deduction, you assume that Parker and Day were politicians and members of the Democratic Party. Because the picture was copyrighted in 1905, these candidates would have been in a race prior to that year. Consulting a political reference book, you find that those gentlemen were the unsuccessful presidential and vice-presidential candidates in the 1904 election—losing to the extremely popular Teddy Roosevelt.

Relying on the publisher's description does have its pitfalls. The church in figure 87 identified as St. Peter's Cathedral, is in reality St. Patrick's Cathedral. Although of interest, misinformation, particularly misspelling, is not uncommon on early cards. Most of the high-quality cards were printed in Germany. Seldom were the views appearing thereon so familiar as to allow a foreigner with little familiarity with the United States to spot and correct errors.

Figure 86. c. 1905. **Figure 87.** c. 1905.

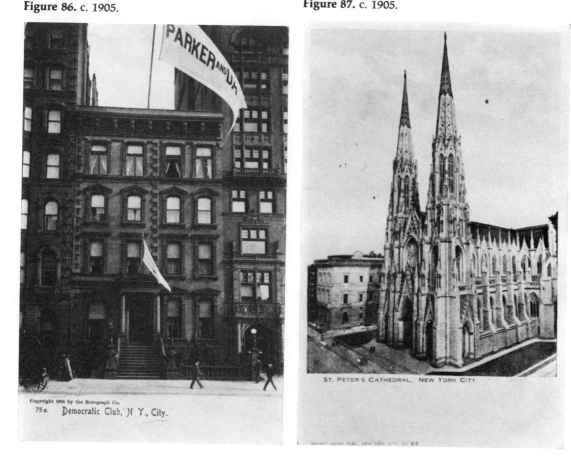

Another bit of misinformation appears in figure 88, a Bosselman & Co. card postmarked in 1906. It indicates the existence of a bridge that was not mentioned in contemporary reference books. The card publisher anticipated the construction of the Henry Hudson Bridge by thirty years! It was opened in December 1936!

Figure 88. postmarked 1906.

Figure 89. postmarked 1907.

The collector should not ignore the written message of the sender in researching his material. In figure 89, an obliging correspondent not only identified the designer of the arch but alluded to what turned out to be the most scandalous murder trial of the early 1900s. Stanford White, one of the leading architects of this period, was killed by Harry Thaw, the husband of actress Evelyn Nesbit, White's one-time mistress. This crime of passion was committed ironically in another of White's architectural masterpieces, the original Madison Square Garden demolished in 1925. The "Tombs" referred to was a New York City prison, which appears in figure 90.

Evelyn Nesbit, the object of the White-Nesbit-Thaw triangle, posed for postcards. After a reading of a biography of her, the date and location of the photograph in figure 91 were determined. The postcard itself is unidentified as to pub-

Figure 90. c. 1910.

Figure 91. c. 1902.

lisher. It is, however, an undivided back, is titled "post card," and has the 1898 authorization line. The assumption, therefore, is that it was produced between 1901 and 1907. The photograph itself was taken during the winter of 1901/02 by Rudolf Eickemeyer and was sold by the Cambell Art Studios.

The Harry Thaw murder trial ended on April 10, 1907, with a hung jury; a second trial in 1908 ended in a "not guilty" verdict on the grounds of insanity, and Thaw was committed to an insane asylum. Ultimately freed, Thaw died in 1947, age seventy-six. Evelyn Nesbit died in 1966, age eighty-one.

Although it is rare that idle remarks written on a seventy-year-old postcard will allude to an incident as bizarre as the Harry Thaw murder trial, the potential of any card's opening up a Pandora's box of fascinating research is always present.

To really sink your teeth into the subject you've chosen as your specialty, you should at least have an awareness of the reference books available through your local library. Reacquaint yourself with its card catalogue and jot down the books available on your topic. Spend an hour or so going through bibliographies appearing in the books available on the shelves, and prepare a list of books that you feel will aid you in researching your topic. Then request the librarian to get them for you through interlibrary loans. Make the librarian aware of your postcard specialty, and ask for her advice and assistance. Librarians, bless 'em, delight in participating in these research projects. They will gladly guide you along the right path. They may, in fact, want to review and copy your collection for the library's archives, particularly if it is heavy in local history.

You may have selected a small geographic area for your study. A visit to the local historical society will be of inestimable value. It too will be as interested in what information you have uncovered as you are in their archives. Museums also have some of the information you require; in fact, many museums have accumulated sizable postcard collections of their own. And, finally, the importance of newspapers and news magazines cannot be overemphasized. Many, many nuggets of information on your topic can be gleaned from their pages. Don't skim over the reports of fires, renewal projects, dedications of new structures, and the like. Often the reporters go into in-depth background data on the history of the site. Mention might be made of the puzzling building shown on a card in your collection.

When

Many of the more popular, and hence more valuable, postcards were issued in connection with a particular event: a world's fair, an exposition, a convention, or another type of celebration. A good many of these cards will at least give an abbreviated description of the event portrayed; the later cards will usually devote quite a few lines on the "message" side of the back. The pre-1907 cards, with the restrictions imposed on the amount of space allotted to a message, pose the problem of identifying the event.

The card in figure 92 was issued at the Jamestown Tercentenary Exposition

FOOD PRODUCTS BUILDING, JAMESTOWN EXPOSITION, 1907.

Figure 92. 1907.

of 1907 and is one of a series of much-sought-after cards known as the *Jamestown A&V*. At the least, a collector would want to know the duration of the exposition (April 26–November 30, 1907), its location (Sewell's Point near Norfolk, Virginia), and its purpose (to commemorate the 300th anniversary of the founding of the first permanent English settlement in America). Larger libraries will have publications on this and the other major fairs and expositions containing maps, guidebooks, and brochures describing the buildings. The information is there for the asking.

The Jamestown Amusement and Vending Company, Inc. (A&V), of Norfolk, Virginia, was the concessionaire for the official cards of this exposition. The A&V series contains 187 numbered cards, which include views of early Jamestown; Pocahontas and John Smith; historic churches; scenes of the Revolutionary, Civil, and Spanish American Wars; warships; and exposition views. An unnumbered pair of cards depict "Army Girl" and "Navy Girl" signed by artist Howard Chandler Christy—both are rare.

A listing of the major expositions since the dawning of the postcard era in 1898 would include:

Trans-Mississippi International Exposition, June 1–October 31, 1898, near Omaha, Nebraska

Pan-American Exposition, May 1–November 2, 1901, in Buffalo, New York (during which President McKinley was assassinated)

South Carolina Inter-State and West Indian Exposition, December 1, 1901–June 1, 1902, near Charleston, South Carolina

Louisiana Purchase Exposition, April 2–December 1, 1904, in St. Louis, Missouri

Lewis and Clark Centennial Exposition, June 1–October 15, 1905, in Portland, Oregon

Alaska-Yukon-Pacific Exposition, June 1–October 16, 1909, in Seattle, Washington

Panama-Pacific International Exposition, February 20–December 4, 1915, in San Francisco. This commemorated the opening of the Panama Canal.

Panama-California Exposition, January 1–December 31, 1915, in San Diego. Also Canal-oriented.

As the popularity of postcard collecting declined, fewer cards were issued for national and international fairs, with these notable exceptions, for which many linen cards exist. Most cards contain good descriptive information on their backs.

Sesquicentennial Exposition in Philadelphia, 1926

Century of Progress in Chicago, 1933

California Pacific in San Diego, 1935

Golden Gate International Exposition in San Francisco, 1939

New York World's Fair, 1939–1940

Of the fairs commemorated by chrome cards, we have:

Century 21 Exposition in Seattle, 1962

New York World's Fair, 1964

HemisFair 1968 in San Antonio, 1968

Modern collectors of an international persuasion would not overlook cards published for Expo '67 in Montreal, Canada.

A final word about how seeking out the answer to one question leads a researcher into wider and wider areas of specialization. Figure 93 is a rather ordinary souvenir of the 1939 World's Fair. Close scrutiny of the picture shows the Czechoslovakian flag at half staff. The description on the back alludes to the tragic betrayal of the Czech people by the Western democracies by allowing Nazi forces to dismember and occupy this little country. The unfinished pavilion, its funds cut off by the Nazi regime, remained open throughout the fair as a mute testimonial to this country's betrayal.

Views of regional and local events often appear on postcards, even if they are just photocards issued by local merchants. These can be the most fun to collect because the event might have taken place "in your own backyard." If the event was worthy of a postcard, it certainly was mentioned in your local newspaper. Consult the paper's back issues for write-ups on these events. You might even find that Great Aunt Tillie was the Apple Festival Queen of 1933.

Any "busy" view card lends itself to detailed research—the cars in the street (or absence thereof), the style of clothing worn by the pedestrians, the buildings under construction—all present hints as to when the scene on the card was taken.

Consider these two cards—both chrome cards of the very popular Statue of Liberty, yet published years apart.

Notice the virtual absence of trees in figure 94, indicating that this view was

Figure 93. c. 1940.

Figure 94. c. 1950.

Figure 95. c. 1973.

taken soon after World War II upon the razing of the U.S. Army buildings of Fort Wood, which shared Liberty Island (formerly Bedloe's Island) with the statue.

Figure 95 shows mature trees and a structure surrounding the base of the statue. Through research, a collector will discover that this structure houses the American Museum of Immigration, opened in 1973, thereby dating this card possibly twenty years after that of the former. Knowing the completion and/or destruction dates of structures appearing on your view cards makes dating the view a snap. How much research you want to do along these lines is purely a matter of your personal choice and enjoyment.

Where

The location of a particular view, at least in generalities, is usually indicated on the card itself. Dealers rely on the description in sorting their material, and collectors take their judgment at face value. Figures 96 and 97 are two examples of the pitfalls encountered in such misplaced reliance.

Figure 96 is what appears to be an insurance company building located in New York City. However, both physical inspection of the actual New York Life Building (in New York City) and a look at guidebooks dating back seventy years indicated that this building at no time existed in New York City. It then dawned on

Figure 96. c. 1905.

New York Life Building.

the collector that the message in the lower left corner of the card indicated not only the possible hometown of the sender but the location of the building as well. A browse through a dealer's "Missouri" material confirmed that this is the building of the New York Life Insurance Company—in Kansas City. Similarly, the office building in figure 97 bears little resemblance to the existing bank building or to any previous building so named. By accident, a card was spotted with the same view, and it was described as located in Richmond, Virginia. Which location is accurate is still up for grabs.

Figure 97. c. 1910.

Although of great enjoyment and amusement, these presumed errors in the titling of the older cards should not be considered of monetary value. The wonder is that so many cards are perfect, as they were printed for the most part in non-English-speaking countries.

How

The final section on research will briefly cover how cards were printed through the years and in what form they were marketed. In the discussion on Detroit Publishing, lithography was outlined—the use of chemically treated stone slabs, one for each color reproduced. This process produced the best cards but, alas, was the most expensive because relatively few impressions could be obtained from the slabs before they became smudged and had to be cleaned and the colors reapplied. A halftone process was invented by Benjamin Day, after whom the process has been named (Benday). The process involves photographing a picture through screens, and the result is different sizes of tiny colored dots. By variation in the size and intensity of these dots, different shadings are achieved.

Cards from real photographs were and still are produced en masse from a single negative that has been made from perhaps thirty or forty individual photographs. These sheets of forty views are then cut into the respective cards, and the cards are packed into boxes of 1,000 and readied for shipment. A section on the various methods of printing, most of which have been used in postcard production, can be found in any good encyclopedia.

Seldom does one see mention of the errors made in cards that have invariably found their way to drugstore racks and collectors' shoe boxes. The relative scarcity of any particular error cannot be determined—but they are amusing to see. The card in figure 98 appears to be a split view of no great interest. The back shows the stamp box appearing in the middle indicating that it was improperly cut and that about two-thirds of the Times Square view (with the Camels sign) was lost and the contiguous view of Midtown Manhattan at night was picked up. The two cards involved in this "freak" were published by Alfred Mainzer (No. 416, Times Square, and No. 490, Midtown Manhattan at Night). The cards bear the logo of Mike Roberts, at which printing plant the error in cutting probably occurred.

Postcard sales in the first decade of the twentieth century were big business in the United States. It has been reported that sales approached one billion cards in 1905. The familiar revolving wire rack for the display of cards has been attributed to one E. I. Dail, who patented this product in 1908. Its use allowed customers to

Figure 98. c. 1960.

Figure 99. c. 1964.   **Figure 100.** c. 1964.

browse through the cards so displayed without the assistance of a clerk. Evidently this unguarded display allowed patrons to pocket a few cards, for soon after (1911), a device akin to a vending machine was patented to dispense cards. When a knob was turned, a card would appear in a little window. Keep turning the knob and up to 500 different cards stored on a belt would appear. Drop a penny into the machine and the card you chose would be released.

In addition to the postcard sold singly, collectors through the years have been offered groups of cards sold packaged either in sets in an envelope or in a number of random views stapled or bound, with the card generally perforated for easy separation and mailing. An intact set in its original wrapper is a gem and quite difficult to find. The envelopes were usually made of the flimsiest paper, bound to disintegrate within a few years. The collector, wanting to display the cards in his album, removed them from the wrapper and discarded it. Thousands of wrappers were discarded as the cards were mailed. It is unlikely that any particular card within an intact set with the original wrapper would be of such importance to a present-day collector that he would break up the set. Certainly no dealer would do so.

This admonition applies less strongly to the cards in bound form. The majority of them have proved to be commonplace views that have also appeared singly. Note figures 99 and 100, published by Manhattan Post Card, numbered NY-97.

Figure 99 is a card from a spirally bound booklet, and figure 100 is its counterpart, which was sold singly. Most collectors ignore these bound booklets of cards because their odd shapes present storage problems. They appeal mostly to the tourist, who can pick up a half dozen or so cards without the bother of picking interesting views singly.

The little folios of pictures, housed accordion fashion, that abound at every tourist spot are not postcards as letter-rate postage is required to mail them. They should be considered nothing more than interesting little pictures.

⌘ 5 ⌘

Collecting—Then and Now

National Clubs of Collectors

A modern collector has to search no further than his own accumulation of material to find evidence of the techniques of collecting practiced by his confreres of seventy years ago. Just read the messages on some of your older cards, like this one: "You asked me to send you a card of the Osch fire as soon as I see one. I will send it to you." The sender obviously struck up a correspondence with a fellow collector, perhaps through a pen pal club, through which they exchanged cards of their respective interests. Messages requesting cards showing courthouses (or churches, or firehouses) abound. For the price of a one-cent stamp, a collector on the East Coast could obtain views of scenes that he would never hope to see in an age when travel was a long, expensive, and arduous task.

As the attraction of postcard collecting reached almost manic proportions around 1907, pen pal clubs run exclusively by and for postcard collectors formed throughout the country. Figure 101 bears the rubber-stamp imprint of one such club. The Post Card Union of America operated out of an office in Philadelphia. There is no evidence that it was connected with a particular postcard publisher, as its imprint appears on a diverse mixture of cards. The club claimed a membership of approximately 10,000 in its heyday around 1910. In their excellent study of the postcard scene up to 1918, *Picture Postcards in the United States, 1893–1918*, George and Dorothy Miller name *Comfort* and *True Blue Book* as publications fostering the exchange of cards among their readers. The latter publication operated from 1908

Figure 101. postmarked 1907.

up to the 1920 s. The Millers also mention a club with the tongue-twisting title of the National Society for the Promulgation of Picture Postcards, claiming a membership of 5,000, which sponsored a two-day convention in Chicago in 1909. None of the early clubs of collectors survived the decline in popularity of collecting after World War I.

The advent of the chrome era in postcards, with the issuance of the first Union Oil set in 1939, prompted the expansion of the Post Card Collectors Club of America, founded by Albert H. Wood in 1934, and its issuance of a periodical, *The Post Card Gazette*. By 1942, the club's roster contained over 700 members' names. The club limped along through the World War II years, with its publication shrinking to a two-page mimeographed sheet. Many of the contributors to the publication were in the military, apologizing that they had to curtail their collecting activities "for the duration." In 1946, other obligations prompted Mr. Wood to turn the reins of the PCCC of A over to two young disabled veterans, Ray Mitchell and Bob Miller, who continued to operate it from Kansas City, Missouri. The *Gazette* grew to a printed publication of one sheet, printed on both sides.

In 1947, the PCCC of A's activities were taken over by Bob Hendricks, an active West Coast collector and editor of another publication, the *Post Card Collector's Magazine*, which appeared in print in 1943. By July 1948, both magazines merged into a handsome four-page illustrated publication printed on glossy paper. Hendricks continued to publish the combined periodical, often at his own expense, throughout the mid-1950s.

Although nationwide clubs with newsletters have had a high mortality rate over the years, they have served one important function—the fostering of local clubs composed of members who "found each other" on the membership lists of the nationals. In September 1947, there were only four local clubs with a combined membership of 150 collectors. Today there are over thirty clubs belonging to a nationwide federation—with memberships in the thousands.

The Local Club

The backbone of modern collecting is the local club, a meeting place for dealer and collector, beginner and old pro. Of the four clubs recognized as existing in 1947, only one, the Metropolitan Postcard Collectors Club, survives under its original name. Founded in 1946 in New York City, the club met at members' homes for the first few years of existence before growth forced it to seek various meeting halls in the city. A handful of its founding members—Joe Nardone, Ben Shiffrin, and Ben Papell—continue their activities in the club.

Often local clubs issue their own postcards for fund-raising or publicity purposes. The duo in figures 102 and 103 are handsome black-and-white drawings in the Art Nouveau style issued to publicize postcard exhibitions. Members of the "Metro" Club participated in both these exhibitions.

Typical of the modern clubs formed during the boom in collecting of the 1970s is the Washington's Crossing Card Collectors Club—known to many as

Figure 102. 1967.   **Figure 103.** 1966.

WC-4. Formed in 1972, this group draws its members from the Delaware Valley region in New Jersey and Pennsylvania, the heart of the East Coast flea market country. Its first president and vice-president, Betty Davis and Ernie Schaaf, continue to guide the affairs of the club, together with Ted Bozarth, who acts as sales manager for club-prepared postcards and as auction chairman. Members of a club of postcard collectors benefit primarily from the information they receive from more experienced club members, from club publications, and from guest speakers who address club meetings. Because so far there is little in the way of commercial literature on the hobby, the clubs represent the primary repository of eighty years of research and knowledge.

The Collector

Postcard collectors emerge from all strata of society and all racial and ethnic groups, and they share the acquisitive and inquisitive instincts of a collector of any type of memorabilia. In the past, when cards were new and inexpensive, collectors boasted of the number of cards in their accumulations. As late as the 1950s, biographical data appearing in the hobby press mentioned that so-and-so had over 35,000 cards in his collection, or 50,000, or 100,000. Modern collectors tend toward specific areas of collecting, as evidenced by these want ads from the current magazine *American Postcard Journal*:

> Wanted—Circus-related postcards.
>
> Wanted—Postcards showing cameras.
>
> Wanted—Any cards of the following Missouri towns.

Granted, the collectors of these specialties or topics would much prefer the older cards that fall into these topics, but every card from each of the eras of postcard production would have their place in such collections. And there are few topics that are not substantially represented among the millions of different cards produced in these eighty years.

A graphic example of the relative novelty of collecting by areas of specialization are these two news articles from the September 1942 issue of *The Post Card Gazette* (italics mine):

> [Member's name] has an *unusual specialty* in cards. He is collecting fire subjects such as fire stations, apparatus, fire views, fire horses, engines and the like.
>
> One of our recent members [name] is *specializing* in pictures of horses, horse drawn street cars and fire engines.

The newsworthiness of the existence in 1942 of topical postcard collectors is truly enlightening, because it is seldom that a collector of the 1970s would consider himself anything but a specialist.

Another manifestation of this trend toward specialization is the formation of study groups. The Equine Deltiologists of America is a club of collectors interested in collecting cards picturing horses. The Space Postcard Study Unit is a specialized group drawn from stamp and cover collectors interested in subjects dealing with achievements in outer space. These modern specialists in deltiology might often use their cards as a segment of a broader collecting interest, using, say, railroad postcards to complement an interest in timetables, routes, tickets, and other railroad memorabilia. A collector's topic can be as broad as railroads, or it may be limited to certain areas of study, such as passenger trains, steam engines, diesels, or a fascinating study of subways and elevateds. Just a sampling of the myriad topics available on cards can be found throughout this book.

With the possible exception of the Mike Roberts firm in California, the postcard publishers of today completely ignore the desires of collectors to acquire interesting modern cards, a complete about-face from the practice of the Raphael Tuck & Sons firm of publishing cards specifically catering to the fancies of the turn-of-the-century collector. This dearth of quality modern material has prompted individual collectors and clubs to produce their own cards in quantity, to be sold at a modest profit to the collecting public. A case in point is long-time collector Coralie D. Sparre, operating under the trade name Coral-Lee. She has produced handsome sets of color chrome cards depicting scenes in the Ford and Carter presidential administrations as well as personalities of the 1970s. Is it too presumptuous to assume that future generations will be as interested in pictures of Olivia Newton-John and John Travolta as we are in postcard photos of Ethel Barrymore and William Gillette?

Clubs producing cards for general sale include two modern clubs mentioned previously, each with plans for ongoing publication. The "WC-4" has produced reproductions, notated as such, of older cards showing trolleys and fire apparatus and will continue to produce cards of a general topical interest. The Space Postcard Study Group is issuing cards picturing space pioneers, including Wernher Von Braun and the Apollo crew of Grissom, Chaffee, and White, who lost their lives in the tragic fire in 1967 at Cape Canaveral. The handful of commercial enterprises that publish topic-related cards includes Roaring 20 Autos (picturing old autos) and Audio Visual Designs (railroads, trolleys, etc.). Club publications and the hobby press are accommodating in publicizing organizations that have produced cards for sale, and their ads include the commercial publishers mentioned above.

The Hobby Press

A weak area in a comparison of postcard collecting with its sister hobby of collecting stamps is the availability of periodic publications. Apart from club bulletins, which in many cases contain excellent background articles on specific topics and cards, there are only a handful of publications devoted to deltiology—none of them issued more frequently than once a month.

In a tabloid newspaper format is *Barr's Post Card News* of Lansing, Iowa, published by Chet and Norma Barr. A mid-1978 issue consisted of thirty-two pages with a good representation of interesting articles amid pages of auction listings. A ten-issue subscription is offered at $5.00.

A publication in magazine format, the *American Postcard Journal*, appears bimonthly and is published by Ray and Marilyn Nuhn of West Haven, Connecticut. A six-issue subscription costs $6.00. An average issue consists of approximately forty pages with a nice balance of news and advertising—and interesting and well-produced illustrations.

The *Post Card Collector's Magazine* is another bimonthly magazine, published by Bernard Stadtmiller of Palm Bay, Florida, with a six-issue subscription rate of $6.00. It appears in a large 8½" × 11" format and averages twenty pages per issue, with heavy emphasis on illustrations.

The magazine *Deltiology*, announcing itself as "a journal for postcard collectors and dealers," appears bimonthly and is published by Mr. and Mrs. James L. Lowe of Newtown Square, Pennsylvania. The magazine is the official organ of the Deltiologists of America, a quasi-commercial organization that has been responsible for the publication and/or distribution of a number of hobby books and checklists. Membership in this organization, which includes a subscription to this magazine, can be had for $6.00 per year.

A recent addition to periodic publications dealing with deltiology is *The*

Postcard Dealer, edited by John H. McClintock of Somerdale, New Jersey. The per issue price of this bimonthly is $2.50. McClintock is formost in the recent attempts to organize clubs and dealers into a nationwide Postcard Club Federation. *The Postcard Dealer* is aimed mainly at those interested in the commercial aspects of the hobby, with indications of the market value of individual cards and groups of cards being reviewed in the publication. The activities of McClintock in organizing card dealers is reminiscent of the formation of the American Stamp Dealers Association some decades ago. A number of national and regional postcard shows have been held under his direction, hosted by local clubs. The impact of these efforts on the individual collector's ability to acquire cards at a reasonable price is yet to be measured.

The Postcard Auction

A feature of each of the hobby publications outlined above is page after page of auction listings. Mail auctions are probably the only source of quality material available to collectors unable to attend club meetings and shows. Auctions are also the most expensive avenue of acquiring material because the auctioneer's commission, sometimes 20 percent of the selling price, plus postage, insurance, and publishing costs, are added to the base price that the owner of the material wishes to get for it. Although all reputable auction houses publish their policies and rules near the mail-in bid sheets, a general outline of the mechanics of participating follows.

The highest bidder, of course, wins the auction lot being offered. Many houses allow the highest bid, no matter what dollar value it is, to be marked down to just a modest advance over the next highest bid. For example, if your highest bid is $10.00 and the second highest bid is $8.00, the lot will be yours for $8.25, a modest twenty-five-cent advance above the second highest bid. The auctioneer will notify you of your winnings, and you must remit the price to him, plus postage and insurance, before he will mail you your lots. The listing of material being offered in auction will often state an "estimated value" next to each lot being offered. These estimated values are determined by either the seller or the auctioneer as a gauge of the card's true value (which in all cases is subjective—what a particular collector is willing to pay for a particular card at a particular time) and in many cases could be just wishful thinking and quite unrealistic. When bidding, you might consider a bid of a percentage of the estimated value. The "highest bids" in many cases exceed the retail prices for similar cards being marketed by dealers, sometimes by as much as 40 percent, which reflects all the "middleman" charges by the auctioneer, who has to pass on to the purchaser the costs of lotting the material submitted to him for auction, the expenses of printing auction catalogues and lists, and the many postage costs entailed in conducting an auction. The collector to whom a reputable dealer is inaccessible is unfortunate indeed when faced with this expensive way of acquiring cards!

6

Origins of the Picture Postcard

The picture postcard, unlike Topsy, didn't "just growed." There is a logical evolution of the modern card from the origin of the first postage stamp for the prepaying of mail, through the issuance by various governments of postal cards to be sent through the mail at a rate cheaper than that charged to carry letters in envelopes, to the authorization by governments for the issuance of privately produced cards to be sent through the mail at the same postage rate as the government-produced cards.

A brief review of the use of postal stationery and stamps to prepay letters is appropriate because this practice fostered the establishment of postal systems used by the general public. With the expansion of trade and the age of exploration and discovery in the Renaissance period, private communications became a necessary adjunct to commercial enterprise. An obliging wagon driver or ship's captain was the deliveryman in those early days. Because of trade relationships, countries found it an economic necessity to establish formal, usually royal mail services within their borders and with countries with which they had economic or political ties. King Louis XI of France extended his royal system to public use in 1524. The royal house of Thurn und Taxis maintained a monopoly over postal delivery in central Europe from this period until 1806.

Government-Produced Postal Stationery

Throughout this period, it was the general practice of the mail systems to accept a letter from a sender with no charge and to collect the delivery fee from the recipient upon delivery. The recipient, of course, had the option of accepting the letter by paying the fee or rejecting it, whereupon the carrier probably tore up the message in frustration because he was paid nothing for his trouble in carrying the letter. Moreover the rates for carrying mail were high and were based upon the number of sheets of paper used in the letter. Envelopes, as we know them, were virtually unused because an envelope was considered another piece of paper and was charged for. Arising from the chaos of the multiplicity of fees based upon sheets of paper and distance traveled, and the uncertainty of collecting fees from the addressees, a system of prepayment of postage evolved in Victorian England through the efforts of Roland Hill. Through the Parliamentary Postal Reform of May 6, 1840, the "penny post" was introduced in England, whereby the sender would buy an adhesive stamp, affix it to his folded-up letter, and give it to the government mail system for delivery. Along with this innovation came the introduction of an envelope to be purchased from the English post office in which letters could be inserted to ensure privacy. The first type of "stamped" envelope printed exclusively for sale by the post office was designed by William Mulready of the

Royal Academy. Unlike the stamped envelopes available through today's post offices, the Mulready envelope's "stamp" consisted of a design that covered much of the face of the envelope, replete with a figure of Britannia with arms outstretched to allegorical representations of England's far-flung empire, and propaganda figures showing the joys of receiving a letter. The patriotic aspect of this postal stationery crossed the Atlantic to be manifested in the so-called Civil War patriotics of the United States.

The Postal Card

The queer coincidence of two individuals' thinking of the potential popularity of a postal card occurred in 1865. Heinrich von Stephen of the German Empire and Dr. Emmanuel Hermann of the Military Academy of Wiener-Neustadt in Austria, apparently independently of each other, submitted their proposals for postal cards to the General Postal Conference held at Karlsruhe in that year. Four years later, Hermann's idea gained the acceptance of the Director General of the Austrian Post and was brought to fruition in the issuance of the first government-produced correspondence card on October 1, 1869. England followed with its first card in 1870. The United States issued its first postal card on May 13, 1873. One of the leading postcard clubs incorporated the design of the first postal card in its card publicizing an exhibition, as shown in figure 104. As can be seen, the design of the government-produced postal cards has remained virtually unchanged through the decades, with the address side to be used only for the address, the message side only for the message.

As we have seen, the idea of a government-produced postal card dates back to at least 1865 and Dr. Hermann in Austria. The actual use of a privately produced card could possibly be traced back to 1861 in the United States, although

Figure 104. 1969.

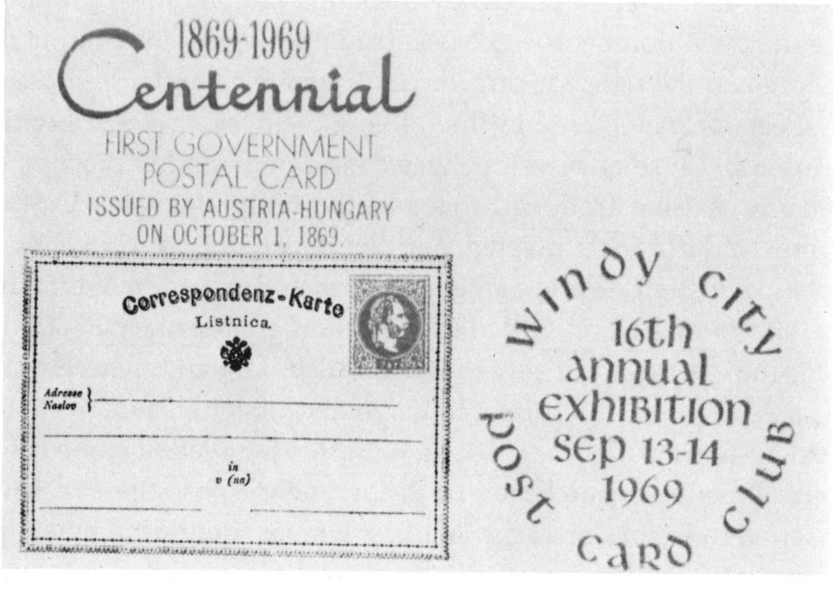

the earliest-known card used postally bears an October 25, 1870, cancellation on the adhesive stamp applied to the card. The 1861 date can be inferred from a copyright issued to John P. Charlton of Philadelphia, who transferred the copyright to H. Lipman, also of Philadelphia. The Lipman cards were true forerunners of our privately produced cards in that they were meant to convey a message on an open card to which an adhesive stamp was applied to pay postage. Lipman cards are, needless to say, exceptionally rare, being sought by collectors of three different specializations: stamps, postal history, and postcards. The Lipman cards were available and sold, perhaps principally to commercial establishments for advertising, until the issuance of government postals in 1873. Government postals enjoyed a virtual monopoly for a reduced-rate message from 1873 to 1898. This does not mean, however, that the U.S. Post Office would not allow souvenir cards bearing a picture or a message (or both) to go through the mail at the two-cent letter rate. In fact, the USPO fostered the popularity of cards by its production of postals commemorating the World's Columbian Exposition of 1893, as in figure 105.

The franchise for the official sets of cards for sale at the fair, which opened in Chicago on May 1, 1893, was awarded to Charles W. Goldsmith. Government postal cards were coated on the message side, and twelve designs were selected for reproduction in full color. The card illustrated in figure 105 bears the official seal and signature of the fair's administrators. Four of the twelve designs were selected for a prefair publicity set and appeared without the seal and signatures. The cards were first offered in a set of ten wrapped cards for twenty-five cents, later at twelve for twenty-five cents. As the designs were printed on a government postal, there was no need for the purchaser to apply additional postage to mail the cards. The fair closed on October 30, 1893. All cards produced for the Columbian Exposition are of special interest to the postcard collector, as they are considered the direct forerunners of the privately produced picture postcard authorized by Congress in 1898.

Figure 105. c. 1893.

Pictures on Cards

There is little likelihood that any researcher could pinpoint the date when an individual or firm thought up the idea of reproducing a picture on a piece of cardboard to be sent through the mail. The evolution of the picture postcard has its roots in other paper memorabilia. In England in 1843, Sir Henry Cole had produced for his personal use a Christmas greeting printed on one side of a cardboard piece that was inserted in an envelope. Interesting, but more applicable to the origin of the current greeting "cards" (i.e., folded pieces of paper) that deluge the mails at Christmastime. Perhaps more of a direct lineal ancestor to our picture postcard is the *carte de visite*, which was all the rage from the 1860s to the 1880s. On appropriate occasions, particularly on New Year's Day, members of high and not-so-high society would scramble from one acquaintance's home to another, dropping off calling cards bearing the visitor's name (perhaps embellished with a lithographed scene, later a photograph) to be accepted on a silver salver by the recipient's maid. This Victorian formality was replaced by the greeting card in later years, when the postman did the walking from house to house.

Trade cards, distributed free by thousands of commercial establishments from the 1870s through the 1890s, bring us one step closer to our picture postcard. Illustrated here are examples of trade cards issued during this era.

The long card (figure 106) advertised the availability of industrial or burial fund insurance through the Metropolitan Life Insurance Company. The small card (figure 107) is from a series of cards showing female figures in national costumes embellished by the flag and a facsimile stamp of the country being represented. This series was produced by, of all things, a furniture and carpet company in Brooklyn! Both cards represent the cloying, "cutesy" design of the era, first popularized by Currier & Ives.

Fanning the general public's interest in faraway places initiated by the expansion of the British Empire and worldwide tourism were the stereopticon slides. No late-nineteenth-century parlor was complete without the stereopticon, a viewing device with a two-lens eyepiece, through which photographs on slides were viewed so that they appeared three-dimensional. The photos in figure 108 appear to be exactly alike but were taken by two cameras spaced a few inches apart, corresponding to the distance between a person's eyes.

People collected stereopticon slides in the 1880s much as color transparency slides are collected today to bring the wonders of the world to the viewer's easy chair. Many, many stereopticon views were reproduced on picture postcards after the turn of the century.

Oh, Pioneers!

The interest of the public in collecting cards bearing pictures, its fascination with things and places distant and foreign, and the success of the World's Columbian Exposition postal cards culminated in the issuance of privately produced

Figure 106. c. 1890.

Figure 107. c. 1890.

cards, primarily depicting views, which were meant to be purchased as souvenirs and mailed at the rate prevailing for letters—that is, two cents—if a written message, however small, appeared on the card. Most of the cards published in this period, named the pioneer era, copied the designs of the German "Gruss aus" ("greetings from") cards that appeared on the Continent beginning in the 1880s.

Figure 108. c. 1890.

Figure 109. postmarked 1899.

Figure 109 pictures a typical "Gruss aus" card, this one showing a scene of Cologne and its folktale of the little people who could be either impish or helpful in their dealings with humans. One wonders if they had names like Happy, Sleepy, and Doc.

Note the similarity in design between the German card from Cologne and the New York view published by a pioneer company, H. A. Rost. Figure 110 was printed and used late in the pioneer era but certainly is typical of the multiview souvenir card available from 1893 through 1898.

The pioneer cards have one aspect in common, and that appears on the address side of the card; they are never described as postcards or postal cards but rather bear the description "Mail Card," "Souvenir Card," etc. A pre–May 19,

Figure 110. postmarked 1898.

1898, cancellation and a two-cent stamp (or a five-cent stamp for international mail) are a further tip-off that a particular card is a true pioneer. This distinction is important because higher values are placed on these pioneer cards than on cards bearing the same design that were produced after the 1898 date.

Publishers soon became aware of the attraction cards enjoyed as collectors' items, rather than just mementos of vacation trips, and started to issue sets of cards numbered so that collectors would strive for completion. The most ambitious of the pioneer publishers was the American Souvenir Card Co. This firm published fifteen different series of view cards of various American cities, regions, and attractions, each of the twelve cards in the series numbered consecutively. Figure 111 is card number "1" from the "Patriographic" series depicting New York views.

Figure 111. c. 1897.

Cards issued by this firm under the Patriographic trademark were sold by the set at twenty-five cents per envelope of twelve cards. (Shades of the Columbian Exposition postals!) The publisher's intention of marketing these cards as collectible items is further evidenced by this legend appearing on the enclosing envelope: "A collection of these cards with views from all parts of the country will prove a constant source of pleasure." Collectors were even encouraged to subscribe in advance for forthcoming series. Those collectors who desired postally used material could instruct the firm to address and mail each card separately, for an additional twelve cents per series, to cover the one-cent-per-card postage rate available to senders of printed matter—that is, cards that bore no handwritten message, only the recipient's address.

The Patriographic series of cards must be considered the first attempt by an American publisher to cater to the collecting instinct of a large portion of the general public. These series appeared in 1897 and within the first few months of 1898.

The full-color quality of the cards compares favorably with that of any card produced in the pioneer era, and the subjects depicted had countrywide appeal. Unfortunately it would appear that its program was too ambitious. The firm went out of business in early 1898 with only fifteen of the planned thirty series having been printed.

Pioneers to PMCs

The waning of the pioneer era was initiated by the political pressures of publishers and the public on Congress to allow privately produced postcards with handwritten messages to go through the mails at the same one-cent rate as cards purchased at the post office. Virtually all pioneer cards when mailed cost the sender an additional one cent to meet the two-cent rate charged for a letter—a situation that the sender quite naturally resented. Visitors to tourist attractions, as well as newly arrived immigrants, were anxious to impress their friends with their travels but were reluctant to pay this additional amount to mail a card that already might have cost them a penny or two to purchase. The groundswell of political pressure forced Congress to act—and the passage of what has been named the Private Mailing Card Act of May 19, 1898, ushered in what has been called the golden age of postcards, which will be discussed in the next chapter.

7

The Golden Age

The so-called golden age of picture postcard production spanned the years from 1898, upon the passage of the Private Mailing Card (PMC) Act, to approximately mid–World War I, when the printing facilities of Germany and Austria were rendered inaccessible. The sobriquet *golden age* could describe not only the exceptional quality of the cards produced, never to be duplicated in later years, but the "gold" that was mined and is still being mined in their sale by dealers to collectors. The evolution of the backs of cards produced in this era is described and illustrated in chapter 3, "The Flip Side." The subject matter appearing on these cards will be outlined here.

This fifteen-year period saw the transition of the picture postcard from an innocuous souvenir of a vacation trip to a collecting fad of almost manic proportions, rivaling if not exceeding postage stamp collecting in popularity. Postcards appeared everywhere: newsstands, drugstores, cutout cards in the Sunday newspaper supplements, card offers on the sides of cereal boxes. The young, particularly, could not resist the lure of the beautifully lithographed penny postcard. Card publishers of the day, many of which had dabbled in the field with souvenir view cards prior to the PMC Act, expanded their catalogues to include topical issues, greeting cards, and sets.

Leading Publishers

The prescient policies of the American Souvenir Card Company attained maturity in the marketing gimmicks of Raphael Tuck & Sons of England, who issued cards in series by the hundreds, together with albums to put them in.

Figure 112 is from a set of six cards, not individually numbered but identified collectively on the back as Postcard Series No. 2327, "Old New York." There are at least five distinct topics appearing on this card that were and still are of interest to collectors. They are historic subjects, New York City, churches, signed artists (the signature of Charles F. Flower, the painter of the scene), and the fifth—the Tuck firm itself. Some collectors would have acquired all cards issued by particular publishers irrespective of the subject pictured on the card. Another manifestation of Tuck's production of cards primarily for collectors is the virtual lack of space for a message on the front of the card—at a time when senders were not allowed to write a message on the back or address side.

Publishers a little less blatant in their catering to the collector are represented by the following cards.

Arthur Strauss, Inc., was incorporated in 1900. Each of its black-and-white PMC back views show the firm's logo—an eagle atop a shield colored red, white, and blue. Collectors were drawn to the card in figure 113 by the presence of trol-

Figure 112. c. 1905.
Figure 113. c. 1900.

leys, horse-drawn vehicles, and the elevated station as well as the white marble Union Dime Savings Bank building. Of special attraction is the identification of this card as being No. 1, the first card issued by the Strauss firm.

Similar in appearance is the card produced by the Arthur Livingston firm in its "Greetings from Picturesque America" series. The Livingston firm had its roots in the pioneer era. The flag in its seated Liberty logo (figure 114) is colored red, white, and blue on an otherwise black-and-white card. This card was of particular interest to collectors specializing in railroad items, as well as church topics, with St. Patrick's Cathedral looming in the distance, its spires dominating the skyline.

Topics

It would be virtually impossible to name a subject (including unfortunately, lynchings) that has not appeared pictured on a postcard. The souvenir view, although considered the mainstay of the industry, was eclipsed by postcards produced primarily for collectors, with little likelihood of their being used in the mails. Foremost among the publishers who produced cards of collecting interest was the Tuck firm mentioned above and in chapter 4, "The Joys of Research," along with the Rotograph and Detroit Publishing firms, which were leaders in postcard production in this period. Examples of the topical cards available in the pre–World War I era, for which there remains a considerable demand from modern collectors, are found in the next few cards illustrated.

The publisher, Illustrated Post Card Co. of New York, combined local views and a year date on figure 115, probably printed to serve as a New Year's greeting card. Large numbers, and large letters spelling out names of towns and female names, were and are quite popular.

Figure 114. c. 1901.

Figure 115. 1904.

Figure 116. postmarked 1911.

Figure 116, published by H. Robbins of Boston, combines multiviews of that city. The topical interest here is the unusual arrangement of the views, in the spokes of a wagon wheel. The large number of views, well over a dozen, would have made cards such as this especially attractive to a collector of multiviews, regardless of the area depicted.

The Ullman Mfg. Co. of New York covered a multitude of topical interests in the publishing of its National Santa Claus Series. Typical of this series is its "United States" card (figure 117) showing Santa Claus dressed as Uncle Sam with the Stars and Stripes in the background. Falling into the three topics just mentioned, it is a greeting card and a patriotic topical card as well. This card would have the greatest appeal to a Santa Claus collector. A card showing the figure dressed in garb other than the familiar red suit is far more desirable. Santa Claus figures dressed in green, blue, or brown clothes, and particularly in this Uncle Sam suit, command a high premium in today's market.

Greetings

The sending of a postcard to wish a friend a happy holiday was as popular a custom in the golden age as sending greeting cards today. Christmas, of course, was the most popular holiday, but cards were also produced and used for Valentine's Day, Easter, St. Patrick's Day, Memorial Day (usually titled Decoration Day), July Fourth, Thanksgiving, Halloween, and New Year's. Cards signed by the artist who drew the design are especially sought after by modern collectors.

An interesting example of the use of a telegram form in the design of a Christmas postcard is shown in figure 118. This card was posted in 1910.

In Living Color

No guide to postcard collecting would be comprehensive without the inclusion of illustrations of the magnificent color quality appearing on cards, particularly on those published in the so-called golden age of postcard production and collecting in the early 1900s.

Plate 1. c. 1907.

A piece of animal pelt and a beautiful peacock's feather adorn these "appliqué" cards produced in the first decade of the twentieth century. Cards such as these were seldom mailed; they were purchased for collecting only. If mailed at all, they were enclosed in an envelope.

Plate 2. 1907.

Cards of this type are generally classified as "American Girls." They are often signed by the artist and appear as parts of long sets, produced primarily for collectors. The artists who created these cards include Philip Boileau, F. Earl Christy, Howard Chandler Christy, Harrison Fisher, and Charles Dana Gibson.

THEIR NEW LOVE

Plate 4. c. 1907.

Plate 3. postmarked 1906.

F. EARL CHRISTY

At left is card No. 1 of the Illustrated Postal Card Co. Set No. 133, of college girls. It was mailed, tinsel and all, in October 1906. The card above is a product of the pen of Harrison Fisher, a part of the "Romance" set (Nos. 186–191), published by Reinthal & Newman.

My name is Dorothy Dainty I started the fashion of wearing Dorothy Dainty Ribbons.

Plate 5. c. 1907.

This advertising card at left, though unsigned, was probably drawn by one of the popular postcard artists. It was distributed by the manufacturers of Dorothy Dainty Ribbons.

The card below illustrates the beauty of the cards featuring postage stamp reproductions printed by Ottmar Zieher of Munich. The stamps, reproduced in nearly natural colors, are those of Germany. The central panel of this embossed card, originally blank, was overprinted with a scene of the Olympic Stadium at the 1906 games at Athens, along with a descriptive text in Greek.

Plate 6. 1906.

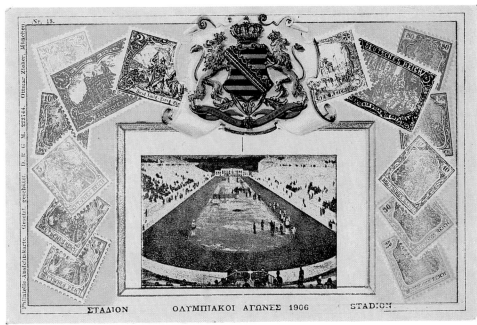

ΣΤΑΔΙΟΝ   ΟΛΥΜΠΙΑΚΟΙ ΑΓΩΝΕΣ 1906   STADION

Plate 7. postmarked 1901.

A set of six giant (six by nine inches) views of the 1901 Pan-American Exposition was published by the Niagara Envelope Manufactory of Buffalo. Shown is a night scene featuring the Howard Electric Tower, which, at more than 300 feet in height, was the central structure of the exposition.

Plate 8. postmarked 1907.

Few cards can rival the embellishments on the postally used card pictured above. Publisher unknown, it was issued for the 1907 Elks Convention in Philadelphia. It is embossed, air-brushed, and tinseled.

Postcard publishers tended toward more subdued colors when this card was printed for the 1939 Golden Gate International Exposition in San Francisco. The figures atop the pyramids in the view below are elephants in the best tradition of Art Deco. An orange glow illuminates the stylized howdahs on the elephants' backs.

Plate 9. postmarked 1939.

Plate 10. c. 1905.

The Art Nouveau movement greatly influenced early postcard publishers. The popularity of portraying female figures with characteristics drawn from nature is manifested on these cards of "butterfly" models. At the top is a card with Italian text showing New York City views, published by Edizione Oxford in Milan. Below is a card published by Success Post Card Co. (No. 1065).

Plate 11. postmarked 1907.

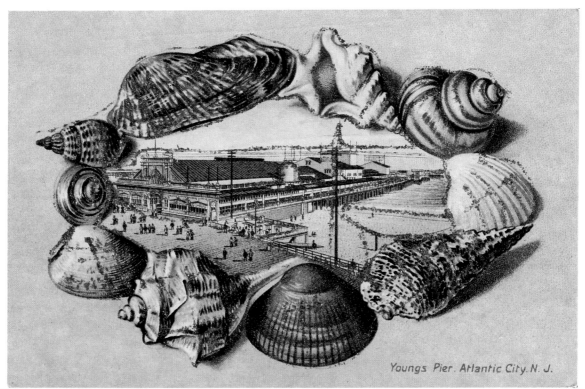

Youngs Pier. Atlantic City. N. J.

Plate 12. c. 1908.

Fancy-border cards such as the shell border above, printed by Lange and Schwalback as No. 442 in their Atlantic City series, display the postcard publisher at his artistic best. The quality of the embossed alligator and shell-bordered cards of another publisher, Samuel Langesdorf, are particularly esteemed. Another fancy border, this time of shrimp, appears below on a card distributed by Douglass Post-Card Co. of Philadelphia.

Plate 13. postmarked 1907.

Greetings from
ATLANTIC CITY, N. J.

IN THE SWIM.

City Hall Park,
N.Y. County Court House,
and Subway Station.

*Dear Marie and Brooklyn. Sept 15 08
all the family we arrived home safely bag and baggage
best regards. Letter will follow. Antoinia*

Plate 14. postmarked 1908.

Plate 15. postmarked 1910.

Popular topics are portrayed on these two cards. Above, a hold-to-light card published by J. Koehler (No. 1505). Each red and yellow window "lights up" when the card is held to a light source.

The opulence of traveling in the grand style is shown in this view of the interior of the steamer *City of Cleveland,* as seen on the Detroit Publishing Co. card (No. 13815) pictured at right.

13815. GRAND SALOON, STR. CITY OF CLEVELAND   COPR. DETROIT PUBLISHING CO.

Plate 20. postmarked 1908.

Publishers of greeting postcards catered to the public's curiosity about the then-new engineering marvels, as is seen on these cards. The top card shows an early telephone, still a novelty in the early 1900s. A flowery zeppelin, with a four-leaf clover as its propeller, served as a New Year greeting on an embossed card mailed in 1908.

Plate 21. postmarked 1908.

A HAPPY NEW YEAR.

Plate 22. c. 1905.

The black-and-white view above, published by The Rotograph Co. (No. A 165), serves as a foil to the night scene published by the same company (No. N 165). The black-and-white view was embellished by a commercial artist with the moon and glowing windows to produce the effect of a night scene. It was done nicely, with one error—the plate was reversed, causing a mirror image of the correct view appearing on the black-and-white card.

Plate 23. postmarked 1909.

8615 "MAMMY"

Plate 24. c. 1908.

It is rare that a collector can find cards portraying blacks and Indians with the dignity these races deserve. Most often blacks have been characterized by the familiar stereotype of lazy, shiftless field hands; Indians by their tourist-oriented "war dances."

Plate 25. postmarked 1911.

These cards coincidentally were both published by Detroit Publishing Co. At the top is card No. 8615 titled "Mammy," to the right is No. 8880, "A Proud Mother."

8880 A PROUD MOTHER.   COPR. DETROIT PHOTOGRAPHIC CO.

Plate 26. postmarked 1906.

Plate 27. postmarked 1906.

Plate 28. postmarked 1906.

Figure 117. postmarked 1908.

Figure 118. postmarked 1910.

Just the dearest baby only __1__ days old,

Weighs just 7½ pounds, worth _her_

weight in gold,

Looks just like _her_ daddy,

Handsome, strong and well,

Mouth just right for Kissing—_you_

Goodness, hear _her_ yell.

Figure 119. postmarked 1912.

A cute illustration of a card used as a birth announcement appears in figure 119. It's difficult to realize that the baby girl, whose birth was announced with such pride by her parents, is sixty-six years old at this writing.

As a whole, greeting cards are ignored by the modern collector except for the relatively few that can be identified as being the products of the currently popular artists like Ellen Clapsaddle and Francis Brundage or that portray a popular topic in their designs—like old automobiles, aircraft, and ships. The more obscure holiday adds both interest and dollars to a modern postcard collection. Cards produced for Labor Day—and if you can believe it, Ground Hog Day—now command prices that can be in excess of $50 each because of their scarcity.

Under the general heading of greetings can be included the many patriotic cards issued during the golden age. Lincoln and Washington were particularly popular for portrayal on cards to be sent commemorating their birthdays. The Statue of Liberty, of course, falls in this category, in addition to the statue's being included in geographic and topical collections. All cards showing the Stars and Stripes fall into the patriotic category. Flag cards produced in the golden age abound in the modern collector's accumulations and are interesting if for nothing more than the number of stars.

Historic

There are few historic events, either major or minor, that have not been portrayed on cards. Starting with the Spanish-American War (any card connected with this conflict is quite valuable), the years of the golden age contained four presidential campaigns, President McKinley's assassination, the Russo-Japanese War, the Mexican border disputes, and the propaganda and action scenes of World War I. Politically, Theodore Roosevelt dominated the scene. Possibly the most popular president while in office, T. R. was amply portrayed on cards, ranging from photographs of the president and his family, scenes during his administration (including inspection tours of the Panama Canal), and his African safaris after leaving office, down to dozens of caricatures and signed-artist cards portraying him as the Rough Rider, not to mention the cute teddy bears, named after the president. During his administration, T. R. sent the Great White Fleet around the world. Comprising practically every capital ship in the U.S. Navy, this muscle-flexing exercise announced to the world that the United States had a two-ocean naval capability. Cards exist showing the ships of the fleet, colored a handsome white and buff. Especially interesting are cards mailed from foreign ports by sailors of the fleet. Collectors interested in naval subjects would do well to inspect military ship cards carefully for their message, stamp, and cancellation date, particularly if the date falls between December 16, 1907, and May 1908. Accumulations of foreign cards might also contain commemorations of visits of the Great White Fleet to foreign shores.

Although postcard commemoratives of all political campaigns are of historic interest, those produced as campaign literature are of specific interest—particularly those issued publicizing third-party candidates. Even the losing-party candidates are interesting because in many cases, their names are lost to memory and are found only in the history books.

Cards used as campaign literature for the presidential campaigns of 1900 (McKinley versus Bryan) and 1904 (Roosevelt versus Parker) are considered rare and hence are both historically and monetarily interesting. By 1908, at the height of the postcard craze, over four dozen publishers issued material for the Taft–Bryan contest. The 1912 three-way contest among Wilson (Democrat), Taft (Republican), and Roosevelt running as a third-party candidate on the Progressive (or Bull Moose) Party ticket was commemorated by far fewer publishers than the 1908 campaign and is hence the more interesting.

Numerous candidates in state and local elections appear on cards because of the propaganda value of the popular postcard. The importance of the election, of course, affects the value of the card portraying the candidate.

Domestically two events stand out as subjects of a multitude of postcards: the San Francisco earthquake and fire, and the construction of the Panama Canal. Figure 120 shows the devastation wrought in San Francisco in mid-April 1906. Publishers, particularly the Hearst newspaper chain, were quick to portray this San Francisco earthquake and fire in all its gruesome detail, the first cards being printed as the city smoldered. There exist many views of the devastated city, most of them at a modest price.

From the destruction of the earthquake, a collector's eye is attracted to that marvel of construction and engineering: the Panama Canal. There are few man-made wonders of the world that can rival the complex series of locks and cuts comprising the Panama Canal, linking the Atlantic and Pacific oceans. All phases of construction appear on cards issued during the period from 1903, when a treaty between the United States and Panama was signed leasing a canal zone, to 1915, when the canal was officially opened by presidential proclamation.

San Francisco under Martial Law, April 18, 1906.
Copyrighted, 1906, by the Rieder-Cardinell Co., Los Angeles and Oakland

Figure 120. 1906.

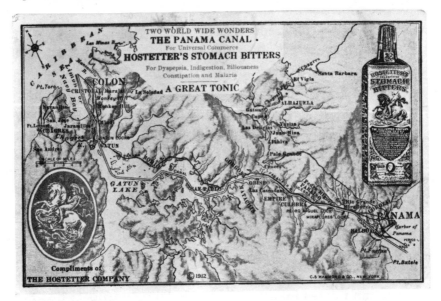

Figure 121. c. 1912.

Figure 122. postmarked 1908.

Dedicating Monument at the Dalles, Oregon.

The popularity of the canal as a postcard subject is underlined by its being chosen as a subject for an advertising card by a patent-medicine manufacturer. The canal was not yet completed when the card in figure 121 was copyrighted in 1912 by C.S. Hammond & Co. of New York, the map and atlas publishing company. The Hostetter Company compares the medicinal wonders of its "Stomach Bitters" to the commercial wonders of the canal in the text.

Postcard commemoration of historic events was never limited to international or national importance. The progression of cards issued by Ezra Meeker is measured more by their ludicrousness than by the importance of the event commemorated. Ezra Meeker, the white-maned and -bearded gentleman near the stone in figure 122, undertook, at age seventy-six, the task of retracing eastward the route along the Oregon Trail that he had followed westward in 1852, in the hope that cities along the route would erect markers to the importance of the Oregon Trail in opening the West. He traveled the 2,630 miles from "Puyallup near Tacoma, Washington" to Indianapolis, Indiana, taking from January 29, 1906, to January 5, 1907, to complete the journey in a wagon pulled by an ox team. This canny gentleman opened an office in New York City to market four series of sixteen postcards each showing scenes of the expedition and the Indian chiefs. It is presumed that he sold enough cards to get him back to Puyallup—by train.

Advertising

Industry was quick to realize the benefits of the popularity of postcards in publicizing its products. Singer sewing machines, Heinz foods, Campbell soups, Armour meats, and Domino sugar are a few of the products still available in the 1970s that were touted on advertising postcards in the early 1900s. Cards showing products that have since disappeared from America's markets, particularly the patent medicines (see above), accord the viewers a chuckle and the social historian a poignant glimpse of America at the turn of the century.

Although many advertising cards of this era were giveaways available at factories, shops, and fairs, one could send away for other cards, generally issued in sets, by clipping a coupon. Korn-Kinks, a breakfast cereal of the H-O Company, offered a set of six cards picturing cartoonlike black people. Kornelia Kinks, a Topsy character, gets into all sorts of difficulties in this set, advertised to "portray the many funny 'stunts' peculiar to the darkey people." One could order the set from the cereal company by clipping two panels from Korn-Kinks boxes and enclosing four cents in postage. Two different postcards bulk-mailed throughout the country, which advertised both the cereal and the card offer, complement this set of six.

Predating the Korn-Kinks promotion by a good seven years, Cracker Jack, the same popcorn product we know today, offered a set of sixteen cards, published in 1907, free for ten sides of its boxes or for ten cents and one box side. The cavorting Cracker Jack Bears are probably the most sought-after of advertising sets.

More ambitious, but of the same "send-away" marketing approach, was a series of 486 black-and-white cards obtainable by coupon clipped from the *Brooklyn Eagle* newspaper. Pictured in figures 123 and 124 are two of the relatively few cards showing subjects other than buildings in Brooklyn, an independent city until consolidated with New York in 1898. One series of six cards was offered each week, from November 14, 1905, through May 26, 1907. The stage personalities, twenty-four in number, and a similar quantity of historic line drawings were dispersed throughout this long set, with heavy emphasis on photographs of notable buildings.

Another instance of the popularity of postcards being exploited in a promotional campaign is the appearance of cards in a publication itself. Known as supplement cards, they first appeared in newspapers of the Hearst chain in Sunday editions in December 1903. They were printed as pages of the paper itself, though on heavier stock, and consisted of seven sheets of four cards, one card from each of four series. The purchaser would cut along dotted lines to separate the cards from the sheet.

Figure 125 is an odd-sized card from a 1903 Hearst Sunday Supplement identified as Series B, No. 2, "Opening Night at the Grand Opera." In addition, Hearst papers produced supplement cards drawn by artists such as Frederick Burr Opper (creator of Happy Hooligan) and Richard Felton Outcault (Buster Brown), both cartoonists under contract to the chain. Two series of San Francisco earthquake cards also appeared in these papers.

The golden age of picture postcard production, because of the popularity of its product, is the most documented of the various periods in the development of postcards. The definitive work to date is *Picture Postcards in the United States, 1893–1918* by George and Dorothy Miller, published in 1976. The cards of this era are for the most part miniature works of art and, as such, were more apt to be preserved as collectors' items than cards produced in later periods, which have been looked upon with disdain by modern collectors because of their inferior artistic quality and uninteresting subject matter. Paradoxically it might well be that there are more cards available to us from the golden age, with its thousands of collectors and collections, than, say, from the linen period of the 1930s, during which the cards produced were so inferior that they were seldom preserved in collections and wound up in the trash basket. A postcard as a collectible item has a validity irrespective of its age and arbitrary classification as being from the golden age. No one can predict which cards available on today's card rack for ten cents or fifteen cents might in time be worth much more to a collector or a social historian seeking documentation of life in the 1970s. No collector should be discouraged or intimidated if his pocketbook or interests lead him away from the golden age. There are still sixty years of cards from which to choose.

BROOKLYN EAGLE POST CARD, SERIES 68, No. 408.
MR. WILLIAM GILLETTE.

Figure 123. c. 1906.

BROOKLYN EAGLE POSTAL CARD, SERIES 51, No. 306.
MISS ETHEL BARRYMORE, WHO WILL APPEAR IN "ALICE-SIT-BY-THE-FIRE," AT THE NEW MONTAUK, WEEK OF NOVEMBER 5TH.

Figure 124. c. 1906.

Figure 125. c. 1903.

8

Exotica, Not Erotica

Much has been said, or at least intimated, of the "French" postcard, the risqué or double-entendre card produced within the first two decades of the twentieth century for sale to Yankee "doughboys" and post-Victorian prudes up through World War I. For the most part, their "naughtiness" would hardly rate the cover of a 1970s smut magazine, much less its centerfold. Their subjects—fleshy pinups and crude cartoons—pall on a viewer after a small sample.

Much more interesting in their diversity are the exotic cards (usually high-priced) that have appeared over the decades. A review of these novelty cards would include the relatively simple, inexpensive cards showing exaggerated pictures and the application of tinsel, through cards on which the sender would complete a message, to the high-priced ($15 and up, in the 1978 market) appliqué, mechanicals, and "hold-to-lights."

The card in figure 126 shows evidence of the name of a small town being applied to a stock New York City scene (Castle William on Governor's Island) published by Hugh C. Leighton Co. Probably the neighborhood general-store owner purchased a kit containing a tube of glue and a bag of metal shavings and then embellished cards by "writing" the "Souvenir of Sidney, N.Y." and sprinkling the shavings onto the wet glue. Many, many common cards have been transformed into an item a bit more collectible by such embellishing, known as *tinseling*. Private senders would highlight an arch or a bridge, the outline of a building or a roadway in such a fashion and mail this special card to a special friend. Tinseled cards were barred from the mails, unless they were enclosed in an

Figure 126. c. 1905.

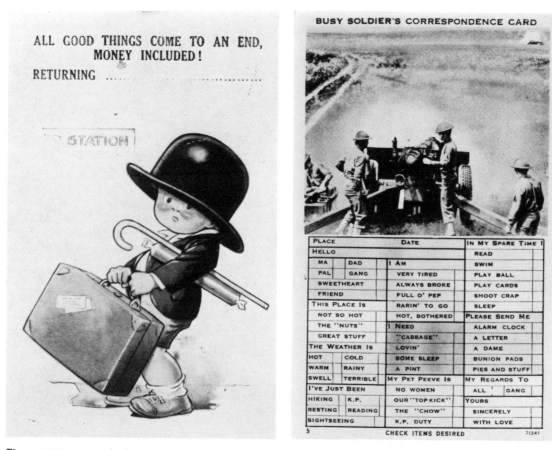

Figure 127. postmarked 1931.

Figure 128. c. 1942.

envelope, for fear that the colored powders would infect an open cut on a postal employee's hand. Just such a case was reported in 1913, when a Brooklyn mail carrier's hand required extensive surgery from such an infection.

Examples of the "write-away" novelty cards appear in figures 127 and 128. On the card in figure 127, a space has been left blank in a message already imprinted for the insertion of the time and route. Other "write-aways" have greetings to be completed by the sender. Cards similar to figure 128 are still published for busy tourists.

Exaggerations and grotesques have appeared on many cards down through the years. Both figures 129 and 130 share the common background of the Flat Iron Building, the first skyscraper, which has been the subject of literally hundreds of different cards. The billowing skirts of these two "ladies" are especially appropriate on Flat Iron Building cards because legend has it that loungers who were clustered on this windy corner on New York's Twenty-third Street, because of the opportunity of glimpsing a feminine ankle, were ordered away by a policeman's cry, "Hey, 23-skidoo!"

Figure 129. postmarked 1910.   **Figure 130.** postmarked 1905.

Figure 131 is an example of a heavily embossed card, one of scores published as greeting cards. Embossed cards can be found for all major holiday greetings as well as very handsome city view cards—some embellished by airbrush. Many collectors limit their interests to embossed cards.

Figure 131. postmarked 1913.

The materials and dimensions used in the production of postcards have closely imitated those of the government-produced postal cards. Cards that vary from this general cardboard material and configuration are of special interest to collectors. Consider these two cards. This 1907 New Year's greeting postcard (figure 132) was printed on a piece of leather. Other substances upon which views or topics were printed include wood, metal, Irish peat moss (what would happen if the card were caught in the rain?), bamboo, and simulated ivory. The scoring on the border of the leather card indicates that it could be sewn to other cards to form a pillow or other decorative household object. Leather cards cost five to ten cents in the early 1900s, and many exist postally used, in spite of the post office regulation of 1907 requiring that novelty cards be mailed in envelopes. Various textiles have been used in the design of novelty cards, notably silk, linen, and satin, some padded for a three-dimensional effect.

Figure 133 illustrates the so-called Skyscraper card showing the World Building, copyrighted by Ig. Newburg. This firm produced a number of city scenes—the narrow configuration giving the building or scene depicted an added illusory dimension.

Figure 132. c. 1906.

Figure 133. c. 1907.

Figure 134. postmarked 1935.

Attachments or appliqué postcards were the forerunners of similar greeting cards available in the greeting card shops of today. Cards showing the application of a real peacock's feather and animal fur can be found in the color section of this book. Figure 134 is a linen card to which a little bag of Great Salt Lake salt is attached. It's interesting to note that this card cost three cents to mail in 1935, when the postcard rate was one cent, indicating that the post office considered the card a small parcel and charged the first-class letter rate. Other substances applied by publishers to a basic cardboard card include coins and medals, human hair, buttons (the "Button Family" series is especially sought-after), and various pieces of vegetation.

Representative of the dozens of postcards produced in the form of puzzles is figure 135, copyrighted 1907 by The Ullman Mfg. Co. There are six flaps, which

Greetings
from
Atlantic City, N. J

12 VIEWS
OF
Atlantic City
N. J.

U.S
MAIL

Letter Carrier Series Copyrighted 1907. Pat. appl. for by Franz Huld, N. Y,

Figure 136. c. 1907.

can be folded in such a way as to cover over the white children. It is hoped that many of the readers of this book are unfamiliar with the term *pickaninnies,* a derogatory description of black children. Other puzzle cards include those die-cut in the shape of small jigsaw puzzles, cards that could be colored with crayons or watercolors, and cards that could be reproduced by the use of tracing paper.

Examples of early publishers' catering to the desires of the public to send multiple views in postcard form follow.

The Franz Huld Company copyrighted its "Letter Carrier" series in 1907. The mailbag in figure 136 contains a slot for the insertion of local views. The card could be mass-produced and overprinted for regional distribution with the name of the town corresponding to the booklet of local views.

The Rotograph Co. received a patent for what it called the album card. Produced on thick layers of cardboard stock, figure 137 contains a compartment of small views, the access to which is a little door cut into the picture and closed with a clasp. Eleven small views of Ann Arbor, Michigan, are contained behind the little door as in figure 137a.

A modern collector might take pride in the "three-dimensional" cards currently available on the card racks. The same process was used in 1906 in producing cards on celluloid by C. J. Deeks & Co. of Paterson, New Jersey. Figure 138 shows one of the Deeks magic changing series. When the card is tilted, a different scene emerges. This view shows the Flat Iron Building and the buildings that it replaced. Another card in this series shows a subject of particular modern interest; when tilted, a man smoking is transformed into a death's-head skull.

Figure 137. postmarked 1909.

Figure 138. postmarked 1906.

A modern exotic card, which has its roots in a set published by Raphael Tuck & Sons over seventy years ago, is the card in figure 139, which can actually be played on a phonograph. When it is played, a travelogue describes the natural beauty of New Hampshire's White Mountains. The Tuck series featured military music.

Figure 139. c. 1950.

Figure 140. c. 1970.

Possibly the only modern contribution to exotic postcard publications is represented in the card in figure 140. The picture is coated with a pressure-sensitive adhesive. The address side is peelable so that the card can be pressed onto a clean, dry surface—like a car bumper. The card, published by Norsid of Yonkers, New York, is numbered WP4, so presumably there are at least three other views gracing the tail bumpers of America.

Mechanicals

The cards just described and illlustrated, with the possible exception of the Ullman puzzle card, were basically inanimate. They were not manufactured of moving parts. Under the term *mechanicals* are grouped the many devices that are pushed, pulled, lifted, spun, or otherwise manipulated, causing subjects on the cards to move in some way. This concept should be quite familiar to anyone who has purchased a book for little children in which, by manipulating tabs, one makes characters move or pop up. Most of these mechanical concepts in kiddie books and birthday cards were employed years ago by postcard publishers.

Figure 141. postmarked 1907.

Representative of the varied designs of mechanical cards is the revolving disc, which when rotated presents five different views in the little die-cut window. The card in figure 141 was published by Wolf and Co. of Philadelphia and postmarked in 1907.

The Hold-to-Light

By far, the hold-to-light cards are the most popular, and hence more expensive, exotic postcards in general circulation. Seldom are HTLs (as they are abbreviated) available at less than $15 apiece. Yet their designs are so deceptively similar to the run-of-the-mill cards issued by the same publishers, that HTLs can easily slip into a dealer's moderately priced stock unknown to him and to many less erudite collectors who browse through his wares.

An illustration of one of these deltiological gems is figure 142 published for the 1904 Louisiana Purchase Exposition in St. Louis by Samuel Cupples Envelope Co. of that city, which firm was awarded the franchise as the sole world's fair stationers. You will note that the upper left corner bears the direction to hold the card to the light, whereupon a die-cut moon and windows appear illuminated in a night scene. These HTLs were produced in multilayers of cardboard, with the top layer containing the picture cut out at strategic points that corresponded to windows, the sun, the moon, and streetlights on the picture. Backing these die cuts is translucent paper that permits a light source to illuminate the scene. Cupples and the firm of Joseph Koehler produced the finest of American HTLs, mostly city scenes, which presented the largest opportunity for this unique decorative process because of their skyscraper buildings with numerous windows for illumination.

Figure 142. postmarked 1904.

Koehler concentrated on views of the following locations, listed in alphabetical order:

Atlantic City	New York City
Boston	Niagara Falls
Buffalo	Philadelphia
Chicago	Washington, D.C.
Coney Island in Brooklyn, New York	The Hudson River

It would behoove every collector of these views to carefully go over his accumulation and his dealer's stock of these locations for HTLs. Because of their similarity of design to ordinary cards, they are often overlooked. As an inspiration, I can relate the events surrounding the acquisition of one of my, alas, few HTLs. After a rather mediocre day locating New York City material at a flea market, I came across team of weekend dealers with a table full of bric-a-brac, among which was a cigar box with, at most, two dozen postcards. Faced with the usual reply to my question—"Got any New York City?" "Don't know; take a look!" (flea marketeers are a phlegmatic bunch)—I proceeded to inspect the handful of cards. The result: a Koehler HTL—priced at fifteen cents! This could be a once-in-a-life-time experience, but hope springs eternal.

Difficult to identify but equally worthy of inclusion in the exotic section of your collection are the so-called transparencies. These cards, similar in concept to the HTL, contain a blank space in a design that otherwise fills the front of the card, for example, a card showing a girl looking into a blank mirror. When the card is held to a light source, an intermediate layer of cardboard with a picture of a devil in the mirror is revealed. Another card style, similar to but in no way as popular as the HTL, is the luminous window card produced by the printing firm of Reichner

Bros. A patent was issued for its process of applying gold paint to the windows of a building, giving the illusion of a cheerily lit interior.

The watchword for inspecting any quantity of postcards is "Know what to look for." Any card that contains material other than cardboard stock or contains embossed or die-cut stock or movable parts fits into the category of exotic material and should be treated with the respect its higher value demands. You might be fortunate enough to get an exotic card at a bargain price. Most times, you will be happy to be offered an exotic card at the going rate and will eagerly snatch it up at the asking price, if your pocketbook allows. As a caution: because even a few of these cards can cost you a good deal of money, a paraphrase of New York's off-track betting system should be your motto, "Collect with your head, not over it!"

9

The Care and Feeding of a Postcard Collection

A serious collector will soon realize that his collection mounts up to a good deal of money—well-spent for the enjoyment his cards accord him. Because, after all, cards are manufactured of fragile paper, some degree of care must be taken to ensure their preservation from cracking, drying out, and becoming soiled. Glassine envelopes or forms of cellophane slipovers have been used for many years to protect cards from the grubby fingers of handlers. A serious drawback of these substances is that they too will crack and crumble away over a period of time.

The Plastic Envelope

There have appeared on the market since the early 1970s polyethylene (plastic) envelopes or sleeves of a size to accommodate most cards in our collections. These "polysleeves" are open at either top or side for the insertion of the card. Depending upon the thickness, or "gauge," these envelopes offer the collector more than adequate protection for his cards and have the advantage of not obscuring the view of the back of the card being protected. As we have seen, the backs of the cards can be as interesting as the fronts. Protective envelopes are being offered by an increasing number of dealers, usually in multiples of 100 at a cost of about one and a half cents each, a small price to pay to protect cards of both sentimental and monetary value.

About the only drawback these protectors present is the amount of space they take up. A hundred plastic envelopes might measure an inch in thickness, which could represent a considerable sacrifice of space in cramped storage areas. A potential drawback to their use might be the "bleeding" of substances used in their manufacture onto the cards contained therein. The use of plastic envelopes is, at this writing, too new to have disclosed this potential damage. As plenty of air can circulate through the opening in the top or side, the threat of condensation appears unlikely.

Storage

Most collectors at least start out by using a shoe box (men's size 12 is recommended). Shoe boxes are usually sturdy and easy to obtain (ask for a few when next you buy shoes, even if you're a women's size 5) and can be stacked neatly on your desk or worktable. You must use a container, shoe box or otherwise, that allows for plenty of room on the sides. The corners of postcards are the most vulnerable to damage. Many excellent cards have been destroyed by being jammed into a too-small box. Also, don't overlook providing for the larger-sized cards, which have proliferated in the last decade. Called the *Continental size* (because they are quite common in Europe), they measure approximately 4″ × 6″, in comparison with the "regular" size of card of approximately 3½″ × 5½″. This half-inch difference in dimension can be quite critical when one is selecting a storage box.

As your collection grows, you'll quickly tire of juggling a desk full of boxes and will consider storage cabinets. Keeping the 4″ × 6″ dimensions in mind, shop around used office-furniture dealers for what you want. I was fortunate to obtain a quantity of cabinets used by a doctor for his index-card files of patients. The dimensions are perfect. Another source of cabinets would be your local library. From time to time, it will replace the card catalogue files, or the librarian might know of a source of some used cabinets. If you're handy with hammer and nails, you might consider making some wooden cabinets yourself.

Albums

Unlike stamp collectors, who know from catalogues how many stamps have been issued and in what sequence, the card collector is left in the dark as to how many cards might be in a particular set. Except for a relatively few popular sets from the turn-of-the-century publishers who issued and advertised their products in set form, the filling-in of series is at best haphazard and a matter of luck. Once album pages are used, you are locked into the progression in which you have positioned your cards. You might have read that a set of, say, Santa Claus encompassed eight cards. You have three of them, so you leave spaces in your album for the remaining five. A dealer, or a fellow collector on the lookout for you, spots the remaining cards of the set, but lo and behold! you are given six cards, the extra one being a card perhaps introducing the other cards in the series. This error in providing for the additional space in the set might cost you hours of rearranging your collection to keep this set of (now) seven cards intact. How simple it would have been to remain with the shoe box, in which, by shuffling the cards, you would have had the flexibility to arrange them as circumstances arose.

There are two general configurations of albums made especially for postcards. One is a throwback to the turn-of-the-century cardboard albums, which had die-cut slits into which the corners of the postcards were maneuvered. These albums might be adequate for modern cards, which are pliable; they are a disaster for the brittle older cards, whose corners would break off with a heavy breath. These die-cut pages have the second disadvantage of obscuring the backs of the cards mounted thereon. Virtually all of the modern cards are completely devoid of descriptive text on their fronts; all identification of the view appears on the message side of the back. Lacking a good memory, a collector would have to remove the card from its slot to inspect the back, with the attendant danger of creasing the corners.

The second type of album page in widespread use is a clear plastic of approximately 8½″ × 11″ in dimension and containing four pockets, selling for about fifty cents per page. All the pockets are transparent, so that eight cards, back to back, can be mounted therein. These pages are of heavy-gauge plastic and can be inserted in a three-ring looseleaf binder. Variations on this style have spaces for sixteen cards back to back, to be placed in an elongated three-ring binder. As this type of plastic album page has been in use for a while (dealers seem to favor it for their higher-priced cards), a number of drawbacks to its use have been noted. Certain brands have been seen to buckle or pucker, thereby damaging the cards inside by bending them out of shape. A bulk order by a card club had to be returned to the manufacturer because of members' complaints along this line. There have also been incidents of the bleeding of chemical substances, as well as condensation forming on the inside of the pockets.

As an argument for the use of album pages for the storing of cards, collectors raise the point that albums are handy for showing off their collections to individual viewers. There is, of course, merit to this rationale; an album in a binder is easier to handle than many individual cards taken from a shoe box or a file drawer. It's up to the individual collector to weigh the merits of both methods of storage and to make his choice. A combination of album pages for your better cards and individual card storage in protective clear plastic envelopes might be a logical compromise.

There are available many, many albums manufactured for storing and displaying photographs. A visit to a photography shop will inform you of the selection. Newer products have pages coated with a sticky substance to which a photo will adhere and possibly, if removed, remain undamaged. *Don't* try this type of album in mounting any postcards you value; the back of the card will probably be left on the page if you try to remove it. Photo albums similar in style to the four-pocket card albums already described might prove to be acceptable, but seldom are these photo albums manufactured in the dimensions necessary to protect your postcard adequately.

The familiar dimestore scrapbook is just that—a book for containing scraps of paper cut from newspapers, maps, memos, matchbook covers, and other paper memorabilia with no intrinsic value, which are affixed to the page by glue or mucilage. This product is no fit repository for a valued postcard collection unless extreme caution is taken in the use of mounting corners and some type of protection for the face of the card. It should go without saying that the use of transparent tape, glue, or mucilage on an unprotected card to mount it in an album is definitely *verboten*. The protection of the card is of paramount importance—its display is secondary. The less a card is handled, the longer it will survive to give its owner the sense of pride of ownership that any collectible accords a hobbyist.

Hurt Cards and Some Home Remedies

Try as you may to avoid acquiring soiled, damaged cards, you're bound to find that beat-up card signed by your favorite postcard artist or picturing the building or street scene that you definitely "must have," regardless of condition. A card with a piece missing is virtually valueless and should not be purchased; cards with rips, creases, and stains, particularly water stains, should be acquired at only a token price and only as a *space filler*, to use a philatelic term, until you spot the same card in better condition.

The main ingredient needed to restore hurt cards to a degree of their original condition is lots and lots of patience; other items that will come in handy are artists' gum erasers, a good-quality transparent tape, ink remover, cloths, blotters, a book of the weight of the Manhattan Yellow Pages, and some container that can be adapted as a humidifier.

A common ailment of postcards is the presence of a postmark on the picture of a card postally used. It was a regulation of the U.S. Post Office that each piece of mail bear evidence of receipt by the office serving the addressee. Through carelessness or vindictiveness, postal employees fed the card face up through their canceling devices. As post office ink is quite indelible on any card other than possibly the modern chromes, don't bother to attempt to remove the misplaced postmark. It won't work, so just live with it.

Try commercial ink eradicators in a diluted form for other unwanted markings. Gradually decrease the dilution if the first formula doesn't work, and if possible, try the ink eradicator out on a similar card that you wouldn't mind having destroyed. For dirtiness, other than ink, use the artists' eraser. You might have to go over the entire front of the card, as an isolated clean area will be as disconcerting as a surfacewide dingy one. A cloth dampened in a heavily diluted detergent might restore a card's brightness when gently passed over its front. The damp card should then be blotted dry and put within the pages of the phone book to avoid warping.

Tears cannot be eliminated, but you can at least make them less noticeable by aligning the torn piece and applying tape to the back. Creased corners, as well as pinpricks, can be repaired by the use of a humidifier. The humid air loosens up the paper fibers over a twenty-four hour period. The crease may become indistinguishable; the fibers around the pinpricks can be drawn together with the pressure of a fingernail. A strip of tape on the back will reinforce this weak area. Use the phone book as a press to avoid warping the now damp card.

With the passage of time, the various layers of cardboard that make up a card—particularly an older one—will separate as the glue used in their manufacture dries out. A little dab of mucilage inserted between the separated plies of cardboard, applied with a toothpick, and a session in the phone book should remedy this. Another way to get some glue between the separated sections of cardboard is to moisten the gum on a postage stamp or a gummed address label and slip it between the plies. Remove it before the gum dries. Enough of the gum will adhere to the cardboard ply to form a sticky surface, to which the other separated ply will become firmly affixed.

This review of home remedies for hurt cards attempts to cover most of the ailments to which cards are prone. Of course, there are cards for which there is no redemption, no matter what restorative remedies are applied. For the collector with these cards, help can be found in the Yellow Pages under "Psychiatrists."

Arranging Your Collection

Although a picture postcard collection is a personal treasure and should be arranged purely at the personal whim of the collector, there are a few helpful hints to bear in mind in trying to make order out of chaos. In general, collectors start off with a geographic accumulation of cards—say, a county. Some of these cards identify the town in which a particular building or scene appears. By use of file-card separators, a shoe box can hold cards of a county divided into the towns located in the county. This collecting of view cards by area is analogous to the familiar country collections of the stamp collector. A collector of cards of big-city views may wish to arrange his cards by topic, that is, by the subject matter appearing on the card, with the cards being sorted into sections for churches, hotels, office buildings, post offices, and the like. Even these categories can be broken down by location for easy reference. An example from a collection of New York City views is as follows:

Churches
 Below West Fourth Street
 East Side
 West Side
Hotels
 East of Broadway
 West of Broadway
 East Side
 West Side

The various subcategories will be dictated by the geographical sections of the particular city being collected and by the personal preference of the collector. There are no catalogues or preprinted albums to which the collector has to conform.

Cards can be collected countrywide by topics. Trolley cars appear to be one

Figure 143. postmarked 1904.

of the most popular of topics. An enthusiastic collector of this topic can research his field and identify the manufacturers of trolleys appearing on his cards. His cards then can be sorted by manufacturer and then chronologically within the "manufacturers" category. This arrangement will be very familiar to a topical stamp collector, one who collects stamps with a common subject, regardless of the country issuing the stamp.

A glance at a dealer's shoe box will indicate just how many topics a card collection might cover—anything from aircraft to zoos. The arranging of the collection is purely a personal matter. Within these pages appear only a few of the dozens of topics into which an accumulation of cards can be sorted, limited only by the imagination of the collector.

Consider figure 143. It could logically be included in not only a New York City collection but under these topics, listed alphabetically:

Advertising—Bloomingdale's Department Store

Artist signed—R. F. Outcault

Buster Brown

Santa Claus—Twenty-one, count 'em, twenty-one

Toys

Trolley cars

The most common of view cards might contain in its picture that old auto, wagon, or trolley that transforms it into a highly prized collectible. A keen eye is all that is needed to spot those popular topics.

A final word about the storage of your collection. You'll want to "work on your cards" at random—when the family is away, when there's nothing of interest on the late movie, when the doctor recommends bed rest after a bout with the flu. Keep your cards accessible—and away from excessively humid or dry areas. Properly protected, your picture postcard collection will give you a lifetime of enjoyment.

10
Exhibiting

If there is one area in which the collecting of postcards is sorely lacking in comparison to stamp collecting, its sister hobby, it is in the exhibiting of individual collections—a harsh indictment of the hobby, but justified by comparisons of exhibits at "shows" held by organizations within the two hobbies.

Steps on an Ego Trip

It is in the nature of a proud collector to want to show off his material to his colleagues. Letting a friend go through his albums, file drawers, and shoe boxes is the first ego-booster, particularly if the viewer is knowledgeable in the collector's area of specialty and can appreciate the items being shown. The owner will receive an exhilarating feeling of pride from the admiration the viewer expresses in this first examination of the owner's collection.

A second tentative step down the path of formally exhibiting parts of collections is participation in club programs—bringing in a stack of cards that will be placed in a projector, the image flashed on a screen, and the owner telling a story about each of the cards so displayed. An adroit speaker will make his dissertation entertaining and informative enough to the attendees at the club meeting so that each of them will be able to relate to the material shown, irrespective of the viewers' individual areas of specialization. At a minimum, the speaker showing his material should preface his remarks with a précis of what will be shown and why he chose it for inclusion in his program, and he should have available pertinent facts about *each* of the cards to be projected on the screen. These facts should include at least the publisher of the card, the era in which the card was produced, and a description of the subject on the face of the card. Fulfilling these minimum requirements for presenting an interesting talk to a local club requires, of course, research. No one, advanced collector or novice, would remain content for more than a few minutes in viewing what is for him a seemingly unrelated group of pictures with no continuity, no cohesion, no unifying element.

So there's the rub—research. What makes this particular group of cards interesting to the owner? Maybe it's the age of the cards, or the scenes, or the publisher. There has to be something that prompted the owner to acquire them, put them in some sort of order, and assume that his fellow collectors will be interested in viewing them. The inclusion of the fruits of the owner's research in his narrative will almost invariably result in a successful presentation and plaudits from his audience. His dissertation might prompt the officers of the club to approach him to participate in a club exhibition wherein different members compete for prizes, one collection against another. Buoyed by the heady congratulations that his thoroughly researched talk has just recently received, the collector in his pride might say, "Sure; what's involved?"

Taking the Plunge

In response to the collector's query, the club officer or exhibit chairman will give him a list of requirements for exhibiting, which appears to boil down to cramming as many cards as you can onto a 22″ × 28″ piece of posterboard. No provision for "write-up," that is, describing the cards to be displayed; no provision for including the research he spent hours gathering for his club talk. Although the rules for exhibiting may vary a bit from club to club, the lack of a provision for write-up, indeed specific prohibition thereof, appears universal.

Figure 144. c. 1970.

Consider figure 144, an actual photocard taken at a postcard exhibition showing portions of four "boards" entered in competition. Nowhere in evidence appears even the title of the exhibits mounted on the boards. Without an exhibition program listing the titles of each numbered board, the viewer may well be confused about what she is looking at. She sees on the second board in this view twenty cards neatly arranged and mounted with photographic mounting corners, some cards showing portraits of eighteenth-century personages, other showing interior and exterior views of buildings. An educated guess would be that the postcards are of signers of the Declaration of Independence and the views are of Independence Hall and reproductions of paintings of the signing. But information on the publishers of these cards, whether they constitute a complete set, the age of the cards, etc., is completely lacking. The board to the right, which evidently won a ribbon in competition, is similarly lacking in descriptive text. The individual exhibitors of these boards cannot be blamed for this lack of information; they probably were not allowed under the rules for exhibiting to display their knowledge about the cards and the subjects appearing on the cards. The fault lies solely with the sponsoring club, which did not permit, in this case, even a title to appear on the board.

To a postcard collector familiar with the rules of philatelic exhibitions, particularly those in which a point system is employed in judging, the current situation in postcard exhibiting is anathema. Stamp exhibits *require* a write-up and give points for adequate knowledge of the material and the subject being illustrated by the material. Exhibitors *must* include on a title page a narrative about what the material presented on the succeeding pages represents, a description of the theme to be developed page by page in a logical progression. Many philatelic judges and knowledgeable exhibitors consider the title page the most important page of the entire exhibit.

Leaders in the hobby of postcard collecting are aware of the shortcomings of the hobby when it comes to exhibiting. John McClintock, the director of the Postcard Club Federation, has graciously consented to the inclusion of his views in this chapter on postcard exhibiting. It is his opinion that a typed or printed description under each card of an exhibit should be allowed, as well as provision for a 6″ × 6″ center area to be reserved for a description of the general theme of the exhibit, analogous to the stamp exhibit's title page. Irrespective of the value of these descriptions to judges in evaluating the exhibits, these descriptive remarks will serve what should be the paramount purpose of an exhibit: educating the viewer in the hobby in general and in the segment of the hobby portrayed on the boards in particular. Too often promoters of exhibitions lose sight of the value of an exhibit in attracting new collectors to the hobby; the noncollecting friend accompanying a hobbyist to an exhibition might well be bitten by the collecting bug if what the hobby is all about is explained to him by a glance at a few well-researched boards. The collector might be inspired to dig further into his own specialty by viewing the results of the efforts of fellow collectors in researching their material on display. The well-researched board, subsequently displayed at libraries, banks, schools, and museums, will draw more of the general public to an awareness of the fun of postcard collecting.

But, say many of those involved in promoting exhibitions, the material speaks for itself; there's no need to describe it. Sure, the informed collector can identify and appreciate a set of Columbian Exposition cards, but will he be able to spot the minor variations occurring within the different printings? He'll admire the Jamestown A&V cards, but will he know how many cards comprise the set? He'll recognize Union Oil cards, but will he be aware of their relevance to the development of postcard production? All this additional information could be presented in a few lines on an exhibit board, thereby allowing the exhibitor to display his knowledge of the material and the viewer to benefit from its presentation.

Judging an Exhibition

At this stage in the development of the hobby of postcard collecting, there is no reservoir of accredited judges to be drawn upon as the need arises, as is enjoyed in the philatelic field. The best deltiology can do is to select experienced collectors who will be willing to spend a good part of their day in the conscientious evaluation of the exhibits entered for competition. The selection of judges may well be considered the single most important duty of the exhibit chairman or committee. A judge, in addition to being informed, should be independent—that is, have no boards of his own in competition—and preferably should be unable to identify the owners of the boards on display. His independence should not be compromised by even a glance at the exhibition journal, which lists title and owner of the exhibit, nor, of course, should his judgment be tempered by a remark such as "Let's give Mrs. X a ribbon. She works hard for the club."

A more equitable arrangement for judging a show, particularly one in which valuable prizes are to be awarded to the winners, would be the selection of a panel of judges comprised, say, of three collectors—each of whom would evaluate each board independently of the others and then caucus to iron out gross disparities in their individual evaluations. From this caucus could evolve a critique of each board, which would be made available to the collector to improve his exhibit by pointing out its shortcomings.

A Point System

To assist a judge in what is after all a subjective evaluation of collections, point systems, first evolved by philatelic organizations—particularly the American Topical Association—are being adapted to the requirements of postcard judging. Again, McClintock's Postcard Club Federation is instrumental in promulgating a system among its member clubs. Quoting verbatim from the federation's correspondence, the system employed by several member-clubs accords points to the following categories:

> PRESENTATION, up to 25 points; Is the subject well represented? Is there a balance to what is being shown, a direction in the way the picture-story is offered?
>
> RESEARCH & KNOWLEDGE, up to 25 points; How much research went into the presentation? Does the display show the owner's knowledge of the subject offered?
>
> ORIGINALITY, up to 25 points; Do the cards reflect an original idea or twist to the subject? Starting with top left card and reading left to right, is there a theme or balanced and progressive "story" depicted?
>
> RARITY, up to 15 points; Are the cards seldom, if ever, seen in general supply? Would they be considered scarce? Age is not necessarily a factor in rarity.
>
> NEATNESS, up to 10 points; Are the cards mounted with care in a straight line? Is the board clean? Is the descriptive wording typed or printed in a concise manner?

In practice, this system might prove cumbersome and in need of revision, but it represents a giant step forward toward an equitable system of judging, giving due credit to the collector who enjoys his cards so much (irrespective of their monetary value) that he has taken the time required to research them adequately and mount them.

As a further device to iron out the inequities in present judging systems, the federation has promulgated an arbitrary grouping of cards by period of production, so that cards produced in, say, 1950 are not in direct competition with those of earlier eras. This device groups cards in these three eras:

Antique   1893–1914

Old   1915–1944

Modern   1945 to date

Although this grouping of exhibits by age is feasible and perhaps preferable in competitions, it does not provide for a truly topical exhibit in which a subject such as the Statue of Liberty is represented by material drawn from the hundreds of cards picturing the statue published by dozens of firms from the pioneer era through last week's chrome. A thoroughly researched board of Statue of Liberty cards, including cards spanning the eighty years of postcard production, should be able to score well in competition with cards of any particular era. A fair-minded judge has to assign equal status to all cards, recognizing their validity as commercial products of collectible interest to the exhibitor. No exhibitor should be discouraged from competing in exhibitions because of his preference for cards of the later periods.

Everyone's a Winner

Many clubs follow the practice of awarding some type of prize to every participant in an exhibition, reminiscent of the sideshow barker's spiel, "Come on in. Play the game. Everyone's a winner!" These multiple prizes not only cheapen the psychological value of winning but give to the entrants of mediocre exhibits the false assumption that their effort is worthy of a prize. Throwing these exhibits a bone, so to speak, although the intent is good, will cause anger and embarrassment to the exhibitor who enters his material in subsequent shows where awards are based solely upon merit. By use of a point system consistently applied to all exhibits in competition, the panel of judges can decide that only exhibits with a point score of, say, 90 and up would receive first prizes, 80–90 second prizes, etc., with no prize being awarded to any exhibit failing to accumulate a set minimum number of points. This fair evaluation of each exhibit, with the judges making themselves available to defend their evaluations to the exhibitor and to point out the shortcomings of each exhibit, will benefit the exhibitor far more than the transitory "honor" of receiving a much depreciated award for just hanging up a board.

To Exhibit or Not to Exhibit

This is the question—though hardly as momentous a decision as Hamlet's—that each collector must decide for himself. Under a point system, preparing an exhibit entails a lengthy investment of time in gathering the required information through research, and perhaps an even lengthier period in preparing the board for display. Arranging for the hanging of the board and its removal at the close of the show is also a consideration. These factors must be weighed against the contribution an exhibitor will be making toward the education of the general public and other collectors in the finer points of the hobby, as well as the personal satisfaction he receives from the well-deserved recognition of his efforts by his peers. To go through the hassle of preparing an exhibit? Well, as the man said, "If you can't stand the heat, stay out of the kitchen."

～ **11** ～
Some Interesting Topics

This last chapter presents a few of the hundreds of topical categories into which a postcard collection can be divided and in which a collector can specialize. A page is devoted to each topic, and where feasible, examples of cards issued throughout the eighty years of postcard publication are presented. Cards with multiple topics are illustrated throughout this guide to postcard collecting. Most cards, even today's chrome, can fit into a number of topics, limited only by the imagination of the individual collector. Geographical collections yield splendid "before-and-after" views of streets ("during," if you happen to find a card showing the construction or destruction of a building). The most innocuous scene can contain a means of transportation, a style of architecture, or a fashion of dress that can make it of special interest to a collector and, with a bit of explanatory text, an interesting part of an exhibit. When a collection is arranged topically, it can span at least the period of postcard production, and if it includes cards reproducing early photographs, paintings, and sculpture, it can stretch back to the dawning of man's desire to express himself through art.

The following pages contain just a minuscule sample of what can be done with cards in the development of a specialized collection. What you, the collector, do with your cards is entirely your choice.

Happy collecting!

Amusement Parks

Amusement parks are of perennial interest. Spanning both the years and the miles are these cards. Figure 145 is a scene of Coney Island on a card published by Illustrated (No. 176–31), postmarked in 1909. Figure 146 is a multiview of Disneyland, published by the amusement park in Anaheim, California.

Art Nouveau

These are typical examples of the "cutesy" style of picture postcards available by the thousands during the golden age of postcards, 1898 through 1916. Figure 147 is a photocard published by Davidson Bros. (No. 406); figure 148 is also a photocard probably printed on bromide paper, publisher unidentified.

Figure 145. postmarked 1909.

Figure 146. postmarked 1962.

Figure 147. c. 1908.

Figure 148. postmarked 1916.

Baseball Stadiums

The home of "dem bums" (Ebbets Field) was abandoned by the Brooklyn Dodgers in the early 1960s upon the completion of Dodger Stadium in Los Angeles. Ebbets Field is shown in the Art Post Card Co. item in figure 149. Dodger Stadium, showing the opening-day crowd on April 10, 1962, appears on this Western Publ. & Nov. Co. card (No. L.155), figure 150.

Figure 149. postmarked 1917.

Figure 150. c. 1962.

Comic-Strip Characters

Many of our current comic-strip favorites had their origins during the early postcard era. Figure 151 is Mutt, of Mutt & Jeff fame, on Star Co. card No. 692, posted in 1910. The comic strip *Mr. A Mutt* first appeared in the *San Francisco Chronicle* on November 15, 1907. Jeff appeared a few years later. Numerous TV reruns have made "The Flintstones" familiar to two generations. Figure 152 is a scene from the Flintstones' Bedrock City in Custer, South Dakota, published by B. Y. Hanscom.

Figure 151. postmarked 1910.

Figure 152. c. 1965.

Commerce

It would be hard to find a section of the country where the F. W. Woolworth chain is not known. Figure 153 pictures the Woolworth home office in Lan-
caster, Pennsylvania, the town in which the first dimestore was opened. The card
was published by Bosselman (No. 8432). Figure 154 was named the "Cathedral of
Commerce" when it opened in 1913 in New York; the present headquarters of the
Woolworth Company was the tallest building in the world, fifty-seven stories

Figure 153. postmarked 1909.　　　　　　**Figure 154.** c. 1913.

high. The card publisher is unidentified but is presumed to be the Detroit Publishing Co., under contract to the Woolworth Company.

Disasters

Disasters large and small have fascinated collectors for decades. A wreck on an elevated railway system appears in Figure 155, published by R. Weigel, Jersey City. Figure 156 is one of dozens of views of the San Francisco earthquake and fire in 1906. This card was published by the American News Company.

Figure 155. c. 1906.

THE GREAT EARTHQUAKE AND FIRE, SAN FRANCISCO, CAL., 1906. STEEL FRAMEWORK OF SAN FRANCISCO'S CITY HALL STRIPPED BY THE EARTHQUAKE.

Figure 156. postmarked 1907.

Figure 157. c. 1909.

Figure 158. c. 1970.

Exploration

The crudely designed card in figure 157 commemorates what, in its day, was a breakthrough in man's conquest of the earth: Peary's expedition to the North Pole. In figure 158 astronaut Buzz Aldrin prepares to step to the surface of the moon sixty years later, on July 20, 1969. The card was published by NASA Tours of Kennedy Space Center, Florida, from a NASA photograph.

Fires

The writer of these two cards used great imagination in choosing these views. Figure 159 is the Windsor Hotel, which was destroyed by fire on March 17, 1899. The view appears on a card probably available at the hotel. Figure 160 is a view of the hotel being consumed by flames, printed and published by H. A. Rost. The cards were mailed to Baden, Germany, May 26, 1899, and were received June 5, 1899. Both cards are private mailing cards.

Figure 159. postmarked 1899.

Figure 160. postmarked 1899.

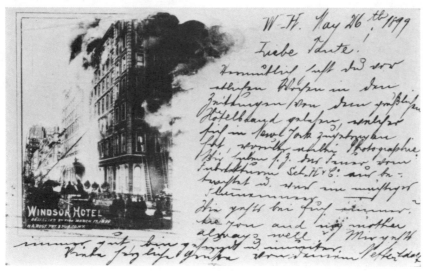

Foreign Entanglements

Theodore Roosevelt won the Nobel Peace Prize for his efforts in negotiating the end of the Russo-Japanese War. This 1905 card, figure 161, published by The Rotograph Co. and unnumbered, commemorates the peace treaty. Though little more than a skirmish, the Battle of Vera Cruz in 1914 was noted by the Valentine-Souvenir Co. in a series of cards numbered around 220160. Figure 162 (No. 220165) shows the funeral cortege of the seventeen U.S. servicemen lost in the action.

Figure 161. postmarked 1905.

Figure 162. c. 1914.

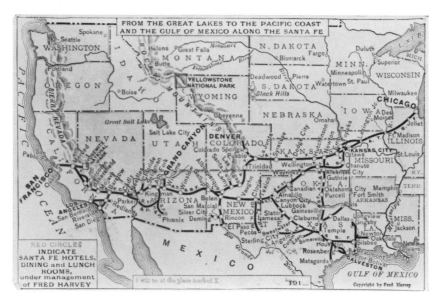

Figure 163. c. 1910.

H-1594   APACHE CANYON IN GLORIETTA MOUNTAINS, NEW MEXICO

Figure 164. c. 1935.

Fred Harvey Cards

For longevity in picture postcard publication, one must doff his hat to the Fred Harvey chain of restaurants and hotels. The card in figure 163, to be mailed during the 1910s, shows the chain's units along the Santa Fe Railroad. Figure 164 shows a card published for the chain by an unidentified publisher, probably Curt Teich. Harvey contracted for cards with many of the leading publishers from 1904 on.

Figure 165. c. 1909.

Figure 166. c. 1909.

39321 The Steamer *Bradley*, which bore Dr. Frederick A. Cook upon his successful Polar Expedition, ice bound in the Arctic region.

Hoaxes

Frederick A. Cook claimed to have reached the North Pole prior to Robert E. Peary, setting off a monumental controversy. Cook's adherents prepared cards such as these to promote his claims. Figure 165 is a real photograph of the explorer by Dey & Dey of Brooklyn. Figure 166 is a card from a series numbered 39316–39322 showing scenes of both Cook's and Peary's expeditions.

Holiday Greetings

Two distinctively American holidays are commemorated by these "signed-artist" cards. Figure 167, Decoration Day, now known as Memorial Day, is honored on a card signed by Mabell Greer. The publisher is unidentified. Cards of the same design but without the "Decoration Day" caption are known. A Thanksgiving Day turkey adorns figure 168 signed by the popular postcard artist Ellen H. Clapsaddle. It was published by International Art Company (No. 51670).

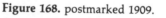

Figure 168. postmarked 1909.

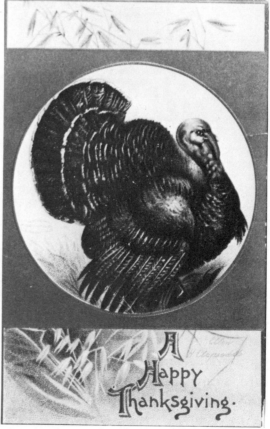

Figure 167. c. 1906.

Figure 169. postmarked 1910.

Figure 170. postmarked 1910.

Illuminations

Modern collectors fail to appreciate the novelty of genuine night views appearing on older cards in which buildings are illuminated for celebration. Note the twenty-minute time exposure on the card in figure 169, as evidenced by the lighted hands of the Metropolitan Life Insurance clock. The card publisher is unknown. A furniture dealer chose a night view of his illuminated building for an advertising card, as shown in figure 170. Both of these buildings were illuminated during the Hudson-Fulton Celebration in 1909.

The Immigrant

The first decade of the twentieth century saw a tremendous influx of European immigrants passing through Ellis Island, most graphically portrayed by postcard publishers. The view in figure 171, by an unidentified publisher, captures the weariness and bewilderment of these "strangers at the gate." The ghettos of the East Coast ports were the final repositories for millions of these newcomers. Figure 172, numbered N.Y. 372 by an unidentified publisher, is typical. The inclusion of a horsecar dates the photo to the 1890s.

Figure 171. c. 1910.

Figure 172. c. 1910.

I wonder if you've ever thought
Of any of the joys denied
To you because we do not trot
In double harness, side by side?

Copyrighted 1908
by I. Grollman

Figure 173. 1908.

Figure 174. postmarked 1910.

A Baby boy

My name is Clarence

My weight is 8 pounds

I was born 9 of July 1910

I have come to stay with

Mr. and Mrs. Alfred C. Tyce

Interesting Usages

A collector will find that any occasion prompted the sending of a postcard during the early days. Figure 173 is a card to be sent to a girl's favorite beau during Leap Year of 1908. The card was published by I. Grollman. The card in figure 174 announces the birth of a baby boy in 1910—the parents being Alfred and Clara Tyce. The publisher is unidentified.

Figure 175. c. 1906.

Figure 176. postmarked 1947.

Figure 177. c. 1970.

Landmarks

Chicago's famous landmark, the Water Tower, built in 1867, was one of the few buildings to survive the 1871 fire. It is shown in figure 175. Shown on cards dating from pre-1907 through the 1970s, it appears with the Palmolive Building on the linen card in figure 176, and with the John Hancock Center on a watercolor painting appearing on a modern card published by Jaboul Publishing Co. (No. 10E), figure 177.

Large Letters

Popular as souvenirs of a visit, these cards are also interesting for the subjects appearing in the letters. Note the 105—count 'em—105 baby faces appearing in figure 178, published by Arthur Martin, posted in 1906. Street and building scenes abound in the letters on the linen card in figure 179, published by Curt Teich & Co. (No. 600).

Figure 178. postmarked 1906.

Figure 179. postmarked 1959.

Lighter-than-Air

The lighter-than-air craft has captured the imagination of the country since the visits of the early zeppelins. Figure 180 is an advertising card of a restaurant with a balloon motif—named after the current (1911) president, evidently alluding to the gentleman's girth. Figure 181 is a rare scene on a modern chrome card. The three Goodyear blimps are seldom seen together because one is stationed in Europe. Published by Wilbur Evans (printer's No. K-19480).

Figure 180. postmarked 1911.

Figure 181. c. 1965.

Main Streets

Mirrors of small-town America, ever-changing yet ever the same. Figure 182 was published by Brown News Co. (printer's No. A-15426). Figure 183 was published by C. T. American Art (No. A-101786). Figure 184 shows a view of Wood Street, Wilkinsburg, Pennsylvania, published by Wonday Film Service (No. 323-D-4).

Figure 182. c. 1910.

Figure 183. postmarked 1932.

Figure 184. c. 1950.

Figure 185. postmarked 1964.

Figure 186. postmarked 1959.

Modern Buildings

In this age of almost total ignorance of the publicity value of postcards, the insurance industry stands out, expressing its pride in its home-office buildings. In figure 185 is the Phoenix Mutual's elliptical-shaped building in Hartford, Connecticut, described as the first of its design in the world. The card is postmarked 1964. Figure 186 is an artist's drawing of Equitable Life's new building in New York City, issued on the company's 100th anniversary in 1959.

Movie Stars

A "fun" collection is a grouping of movie stars' homes—particularly if the same home has been occupied by more than one star (at different times, it is hoped). Figures 187 and 188 are two linen cards from a long set published by Longshaw Card Co. and picture two of the screen's revered performers: Clark Gable and Judy Garland.

Figure 187. postmarked 1949.

Figure 188. postmarked 1948.

Figure 189. c. 1910.

Figure 190. c. 1910.

Natural Wonders

Unrivaled in its beauty, Niagara Falls appears on many cards. Figure 189 shows the frozen falls and an ice mountain formed by tons of spray published by H. H. Tammen Co. (No. 5111). In figure 190 the giant redwood "Wawona" bridges the trail on which a troop of cavalry pass (No. 2203). The publisher, Edward H. Mitchell, has used this view for many cards, with wagons and autos going through the tree.

Richard M. Nixon

Memorabilia of the Nixon administration might prove to be one of the "hot" topics. Figure 191 is a card published during the Nixon presidency by C. A. Novelty Co. (printer's No. K-8594). Figure 192 is a satirical memento of the Senate investigating committee whose disclosures led to the resignation of the president in 1974. Shown are Nixon and Senator Sam Ervin—and the famous Watergate tapes. The card was published by Triple T Novelty Co.

Figure 191. c. 1968.

Figure 192. c. 1974.

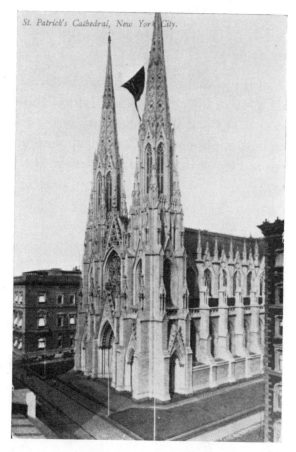

Figure 193. c. 1910.

Figure 194. postmarked 1913.

Old Glory

Many collectors specialize in cards picturing the national flag, in both natural and exaggerated form. Old Glory appears suspended between the spires of St. Patrick's Cathedral on the card in figure 193, published by Rosin & Co. (No. 578). A huge flag—out of scale, as are most of the pedestrians appearing on the card in figure 194—dwarfs the diminutive Old Custom House at Monterey, California. The card was published by Edward H. Mitchell (No. 160) and posted in 1913.

Frederick B. Opper

Considered one of the giants of cartoon art, Frederick Burr Opper has lent his work to many cards. One of his characters—Happy Hooligan—appears in figure 195, published by Raphael Tuck & Sons from its series of Valentine Post Cards (No. 5). His early characters, Alphonse and Gaston, appear on the supplement card in figure 196, given free to Hearst newspaper readers in the Sunday editions.

Figure 195. postmarked 1908.

Figure 196. c. 1906.

Political Also-Rans

Representative of the hundreds of political campaign cards is figure 197, a 1908 card boosting the candidacy of William Jennings Bryan. Figure 198, from the same campaign, is the far more interesting political card of a third party. Incidentally William Howard Taft won the election.

Figure 197. 1908.

Figure 198. postmarked 1908.

Presidents

Contrast this turn-of-the-century card showing Teddy Roosevelt as the current president with the card in figure 200 issued during the Jimmy Carter administration. Figure 199 was printed after 1907, publisher unidentified. Figure 200 is a card advertising a thirty-eight-card series showing portraits of the presidents by artist Morris Katz. Many of this artist's paintings have been reproduced on picture postcards.

Figure 199. 1901.

Figure 200. 1977.

Religious Holidays

Often appearing on postcards are religious themes like the Jewish New Year, figure 201, on a Williamsburg Post Card Co. issue. The familiar Protestant observance of Rally Day, celebrated to boost church attendance, is announced on the card in figure 202, published by Goodenough & Woglom Co.

Figure 202. c. 1910.

תַּשְׁלִיךְ

וְתַשְׁלִיךְ בִּמְצֻלוֹת יָם כָּל חַטֹאתָם
לְשָׁנָה טוֹבָה תִּכָּתֵבוּ

Figure 201. c. 1910.

Ships out of Water

In figure 203 a model warship of World War I vintage, the USS *Recruit*, was placed in a popular park to serve as a reminder of the need for recruits for the armed forces. The card was published by American Art (No. R-77864). Figure 204 shows the venerable USS *Texas*, veteran of two world wars, resting in Texas near the San Jacinto Monument, site of the Battle of San Jacinto. The card was published by Color-King (printer's No. 16198).

Figure 203. c. 1915.

Figure 204. c. 1915.

Figure 205. c. 1910.

Figure 206. c. 1910.

Skyscrapers

Skyscrapers hold a fascination for many collectors countrywide. Note the application of the term to Indian tepees in figure 205, published by W. T. Ridgley Calendar Co. as part of its Western series. The view in figure 206 appeared on the cover of the 1915 edition of *King's Views of New York* as an artist's conception of the future. Note the aircraft and the elevated trains. The card was produced by the H. H. Tammen Co. (No. N.Y.11).

Submarines

Figure 207 shows that the submarine was just a novelty when this pre–World War I view was taken at Newport, Rhode Island, showing the submarines *Shark* and *Porpoise*, as exemplified by the message on the back of the card, "... see these funny little boats. They go way down under the water, men & all, & then shoot up again." The card was published by Metropolitan News & Publishing Co. (No. G.15071). Figure 208, a card by an unidentified publisher, shows two of these "funny little boats" in dry dock at the Brooklyn Navy Yard.

Figure 207. postmarked 1909.

Figure 208. c. 1905.

Figure 209. postmarked 1906.

Figure 210. c. 1930.

Superlatives

The largest, the smallest, the longest, the shortest ... always interesting. Port Los Angeles, just emerging from its frontier days, is shown in figure 209. The sender states "the wharf looks exactly like that picture." C. T. American Art published this view of the largest chair in the world (No. A-50765) in figure 210.

An interesting specialty in a "superlative" topic is exemplified by these cards—from different cities but boasting of the size of their respective buildings "outside of New York City." Figure 211 is a card published by the Feicke-Desch Printing Co. for the city of Cincinnati. It was posted in 1915. The card in figure 212 was published for the New Seattle Chamber of Commerce and posted 1913. The publisher is unidentified but it probably was Detroit Publishing, under contract.

Figure 211. postmarked 1915.

Figure 212. postmarked 1913.

Swimming

A study in contrasts. In figure 213 a crowd of women and girls taking a break from the sweltering streets of New York's East Side at one of the public pools is shown on a Rotograph card (No. A148a). The enclosed pool of a New Jersey inn is portrayed on the card in figure 214, by Bill Bard Associates (printer's No. 100434).

Figure 213. postmarked 1911.

Figure 214. c. 1960.

Touring

The versatile card in figure 215, published by Illustrated (No. 96-50), is a New York City view, but by overprinting, it was used to publicize many areas in the East. Note "From Bridgeport to Savin Rock, Conn." in the message space in figure 216. Both cards, coincidentally, were posted in July 1908, one from New York, the other from Bridgeport.

Figure 215. postmarked 1908.

Figure 216. postmarked 1908.

Tragedy

Postcard publishers were quick to commemorate the assassination of President William McKinley. Figure 217 (publisher unidentified) reproduces what is probably the last photograph of the president before his death. In figure 218 the scene of the assassination is shown on this "divided-back" card (publisher unidentified, No. A-9335), which was produced at least five years after the event.

Figure 217. 1901.

Figure 218. c. 1907.

Transportation

Collectors of all eras of postcard production are interested in forms of transportation—the odder the better. An incongruous scene of a covered wagon on a modern city street was captured in figure 219, published by Ezra Meeker in his Oregon Trail Monument Expedition series (No. A-15607). Figure 220 is an advertising card for a motorized scooter! The text on the back advertises 100 miles on one gallon of gasoline, just the thing for an energy-conscious nation. The manufacturer of this marvel was Keeler-Blakeney Inc. The card was posted in New York in July 1917.

Figure 219. c. 1907.

Figure 220. postmarked 1917.

Trolleys

Probably the most popular topic appearing on cards!

Figure 221 shows a Danbury, Connecticut, street scene, with a flag-festooned building decorated for an Odd Fellows meeting. This card was published by American News (No. B 13097). Figure 222 shows an unusual double-decker trolley that appeared on New York City streets in 1912. Of an experimental nature, it was not in service for a very long time. The card was published by American Art (No. R-40495).

Figure 221. c. 1908.

Figure 222. c. 1912.

Figure 223. c. 1917.

Figure 224. postmarked 1944.

War Patriotics

Soldiers' mail from the two world wars shows the respective Allies' flags. Figure 223 was published by Illustrated Postal Card & Nov. Co. and mailed from France by a "doughboy" during World War I. Figure 224 is a card printed by Maxwell, Love & Co. Ltd. of London and mailed by a "GI" on February 12, 1944.

The War Plane

America's involvement in World War I occurred too late for the participation of her home-produced aircraft. Not so with World War II, in which thousands of these B-17s were flown in all theatres of the war. Figure 225 shows card No. AP8, one of a ten-subject Army Airplane series published by Tichnor Bros. The current workhorse of America's air arsenal, the B-52, is shown in figure 226, published by Upper Michigan Card Co. (printer's No. 96702).

Figure 225. c. 1945.

Figure 226. c. 1965.

World War I

New York's Fifth Avenue is the traditional parade thoroughfare for military reviews. The photocard in figure 227, published by W. W. Brooks, shows a regiment of doughboys on their way to France in August 1917. Figure 228 is a scene of a huge victory parade welcoming home the troops on March 25, 1919. It is from an unnumbered series of photocards published by Photo Roto, Inc.

Figure 227. 1917.

Figure 228. postmarked 1919.

Appendix
Postcard Collectors' Clubs

Over thirty clubs were associated with the Postcard Club Federation as of mid-1978. Because the mailing addresses of these clubs change from time to time as members are elected to secretarial posts, the clubs' current addresses have been omitted. To inquire about the existence of a federation-associated club in your area, write:

Postcard Club Federation
John H. McClintock, Director
Box 27
Somerdale, New Jersey 08083

A stamped envelope with your return address should accompany all inquiries.
The geographical breakdown, by state, appears below:

Alabama
    Exposition Postcard Collectors Club
California
    Angels Flight Postcard Club
    Golden Gate Postcard Club
Delaware
    First State Postcard Club
Florida
    Sunshine Postcard Club
Illinois
    Windy City Postcard Club
Indiana
    Maple City Postcard Club
Iowa
    Post Card Pals
Maryland
    Monumental Postcard Club
Massachusetts
    Bay State Postcard Club
Minnesota
    Twin City Postcard Club
Missouri
    Gateway Postcard Club
New Jersey
    Chrome Card Collectors Club
    Garden State Postcard Club
    South Jersey Postcard Club

New York
    Central New York Postcard Club
    Cuba-International Postcard Club
    Great South Bay Postcard Club
    Metropolitan Postcard Collectors Club
    Postcard Collectors Club of Buffalo
    Upstate New York Postcard Club
    Western New York Postcard Club
Ohio
    Western Reserve Postcard Society
Oregon
    Webfooters Postcard Club
Pennsylvania
    Deltiologists of America
    Morlattan Postcard Club
    The Postcard Club
    Washington's Crossing Card Collectors Club
Rhode Island
    Rhode Island Postcard Club
Washington
    Equine Deltiologists of America

Glossary

As with all disciplines of study, a specialized language has evolved over the decades to describe postcards and the hobby of collecting them. Terms unfamiliar to the layman's ears are used throughout this book. Most are self-explanatory when taken in context. A few are listed in glossary form below.

deltiologist   one who collects and studies picture postcards.

deltiology   the study of postcards. Taken from the Greek *deltion*, meaning "small writing tablet," and *logos*, "the study of."

postal cards   the cards issued by world governments, available at post offices, to which no additional postage need be affixed to be sent through the mails.

postcard   a privately produced card, usually of the same dimensions as a government postal card, to which postage in some form must be applied for mailing.

postcard back   the "address" side of the card bearing the postage. *Undivided backs* describes cards produced prior to March 1, 1907, the first date when senders could write a message on the back of privately produced postcards.

For ease in categorizing cards by age, these "eras" have been arbitrarily established:

pioneer era (1893–1897)   Spanning the years from the issuance of picture *postal* cards by the U.S. Post Office for sale at the World's Columbian Exposition in Chicago, to the Private Mailing Card Act of Congress of May 19, 1898. The backs of the privately produced cards in this era often bear the title "Souvenir Card" or "Mail Card."

private mailing card (PMC) era (1898–1901)   Privately produced cards, authorized by Congress, were titled *private mailing cards* (PMCs) from passage of the act through December 24, 1901.

post card era (1901–1907)   Congress authorized use of the term *post card* on privately produced cards after December 24, 1901.

divided-back era (1907–1914)   Writing was permitted on the left portion of a postcard back on March 1, 1907.

white bordered era (1915–1930)   World War I cut off supplies of the beautifully colored German printed cards that were contracted for by U.S. publishers. Domestic printers stinted on ink costs by introducing wide, colorless borders around the pictures on the fronts of the cards.

linen era (1930–1944)   Postcards issued on high-rag-content stock that allowed the use of cheap gaudy inks. *Linen* refers to the texturelike feel of the cardboard stock.

chrome era (1945 to date)   The familiar glossy color photograph of today's cards, now employed almost exclusively in the commercial printing of postcards.

Bibliography

Books and Articles

Bourcey-Beckley, W. *The Post-Card Handbook.* Published by the author. Los Angeles, California 1954.

Bozarth, Theodore W. *Origins of Post Cards* (monograph), appearing in *S.P.A. Journal* (February 1975).

Burdick, J. R. *Pioneer Postcards.* New York: Nostalgia Press, 1958.

Klamkin, Marian. *Picture Postcards.* New York: Dodd, Mead & Company, 1974.

Lackey, Bernard B. *Handbook for the Issues of Edw. H. Mitchell, Publisher.* Published by the author. Box 1426, North Springfield, Virginia 22151, date unknown.

Lewis, Betty. *Monterey Bay Yesterday.* Fresno Valley Publishers, 1977.

Miller, George and Dorothy. *Picture Postcards in the United States, 1893–1918.* New York: Clarkson N. Potter, Inc., 1976.

Publications of Postcard Collector Organizations

American Postcard Journal, Box 562, West Haven, Connecticut 06516.

Deltiology, Deltiologists of America, 3709 Gradyville Road, Newtown Square, Pennsylvania 19073.

The Maple City Post Card Club Bulletin, Box 644, Elkart, Indiana 46515.

Metro News, The Metropolitan Post Card Collectors Club, 16-08 212th Street, Bayside, New York 11360.

Post Card Collector's Magazine, Box 184, Palm Bay, Florida 32905.

The Post Card Dealer, Box 27, Somerdale, New Jersey 08083.

Washington's Dispatch, Washington's Crossing Card Collectors Club, Box 39, Washington's Crossing, Pennsylvania 18977.

What Cheer News, Rhode Island Post Card Club, 20 Asher Avenue, Pawcatuck, Connecticut 06379.

About the Author

Born, raised, and educated in New York City, THOMAS E. RANGE has combined his lifelong interest in stamp collecting with his fondness for his hometown by applying his philatelic skills in researching subjects appearing on stamps to the fascinating views caught in the camera's-eye, which have been reproduced on picture postcards during the last eighty years. Items from his extensive and thoroughly researched collection of picture postcards of New York City have been used as illustrations for his series of historical articles that appeared in the *World Trade Community News*, a Manhattan newspaper, over a two-year period. He is a member of numerous stamp and postcard collectors' clubs.

After living for more than thirty-five years in New York, Mr. Range now resides with his wife and five children in Bucks County, Pennsylvania, commuting each day to his office in downtown Manhattan, where he holds a position as a financial officer in an investment company.